Date Loaned

11/7/03			

1054

1054

Padre Pio

Books by Oscar De Liso

GOD'S THUMB DOWN
WHEAT OF NIGHT
PADRE PIO

PADRE
PIO The Priest Who Bears
the Wounds of Christ

Oscar De Liso

McGraw-Hill Book Company, Inc.
New York   Toronto   London

PADRE PIO

Library of Congress Catalog Card Number: 60-15686

First Edition

16242

Author's note: Conforming with the decrees of Urban VIII, I
hereby declare that in narrating extraordinary facts and in
passing moral judgments I do not wish to give these pages any
other value than those values usually attributed to other his-
torical narratives. It is not my intention to anticipate in any way
the decisions of the Roman Catholic Church.

For my daughter Monica

Chapter 1

PADRE PIO, possibly the first priest in history to have the stigmata, bleeds from open wounds in his hands, in his side, and in his feet. His side wound spills two ounces of blood a day. It's a cut shaped like an upside down cross, the vertical line vanishing as a light mark at the end. The wounds in his palms go through his hands. They are festered holes of red and brown membranes, but present no inflammation of the tissues. The flesh is alive. Even a slight pressure causes a great deal of pain. The wounds in his feet are wider on top. The stigmata befell him on the morning of September 20, 1918.

When the stigmata appeared, he was put under medical observation at once. For months, only doctors were allowed to seal and unseal his bandages. But although various doctors at different times have tried to heal him since 1918, the wounds have never closed and his pains have never been alleviated.

Padre Pio is seventy-three years old. He bears the stamp of age lightly on his face—a face composed, peaceable, and enduring. Under the wide collar of his robe a part of his shoulder is visible. The skin is smooth and clear without marks of age. His expression is above all deeply reflective, although at times it bears a look of profound fatigue.

Padre Pio looks to be in good health. He seems taller than his five feet ten inches, and although his weight is 165 pounds, he looks heavier. But out of the brown bandages and half gloves which he wears tightly bound around his palms, his fingers, finely tapered, look extremely fragile and seem weightless.

His enduring, composed face, his dark and vivid eyes, his white, curly beard, his heavy shoulders in the brown robe, the gloved hands, the delicate fingers which do not seem to belong to him, can be seen all day long in the confessional box in the little church of Saint Mary of the Graces. All day long people crowd the church to watch Padre Pio.

He seems perfectly oblivious of the crowd in the church as he sits in the confessional. He sits relaxed, comfortable in his Franciscan robe with the wide cowl, the white sash. The expression on his face is completely attentive as he listens. He concentrates on the confession, leaning his head now to one side and now to the other, his hands turning to adjust the little doors as though he were modulating the voices. In his hands he holds a flat metal box the size of an aspirin box, which contains granulated cedarwood herbs. The odor pleases him.

The church of Saint Mary of the Graces is 435 years old. It is a countryside church. Its two unadorned rooms can barely accommodate two hundred people. But it is an airy church. Its spotless floors and walls and high ceiling give it a quality of spaciousness. Recently, at a cost of a few thousand lire, it was redesigned, and its fresh new façade looks cheerful. On the right of the church is the monastery—the Capuchin monastery of San Giovanni Rotondo. It sits on the high Gargano Mountains, above Foggia, overlooking the Gulf of Manfredonia in Italy's deep South. In contrast to the newly restored church, the whitewashed monastery looks old indeed. Its garden wall of local, uncut stones needs repairs.

To reach the monastery, pilgrims climb a mile and a half from the town of San Giovanni Rotondo on a wide, well-kept mountain road bordered with flowers. It is a beautiful road, lined with a profusion of magnolia trees. It leads to a cobblestone clearing just below the top of the Gargano Mountains. In the clearing, almost directly in front of the monastery door, stands a single elm tree.

The clearing is not large, yet fifteen thousand people crowded into it on May 5, 1956 for the inauguration of the House for the Relief of Suffering. Built next door to the monastery, this is a hospital with five hundred beds, four surgery rooms, a clinic for children, a pharmaceutical department, twenty-four doctors, eighty nurses, and a department for training nurses. The magnificent building, seven stories high, is constructed of beautiful pink stone. Its floors are of costly Carrara marble, with red Carso marble in the foyers, and green marble on the stairways. The building has air conditioning, a large library, and an auditorium where movies are shown. This magnificent edifice was realized with donations to Padre Pio. It cost five million dollars.

The official name of the hospital is The Fiorello La Guardia Clinic. In 1947 Fiorello La Guardia, the former Mayor of New York, Director-General of UNRRA in 1946, provided 340 thousand dollars from unused UNRRA funds to start the construction.

The air is high mountain air, 4000 feet above sea level. In the deep silence of early morning, Saint Mary of the Graces, the monastery, and the House for the Relief of Suffering seem nestled peacefully beneath nearby Monte Calbo, an utterly naked, burnt mountain of barren red rock.

Every day in the year, also in the snow and in the fierce wind from the Adriatic Sea, pilgrims arrive early in the morning, whole families in buses and in overloaded cars. At the end of the well-graveled road which climbs gently from the town of San Giovanni Rotondo, the vehicles quietly park around the elm tree.

Pilgrims, waiting for their turn to be confessed by Padre Pio, sit beneath the elm tree. From there they can see a seemingly endless chain of hills and plains below them, all the way to Manfredonia down by the sea. They have come from all regions of Italy and from abroad as well—Paris, London, New York. While they wait they visit the monastery, a low, two-storied structure with a single high-arched, gray-painted door. The garden wall, where it still stands, is six feet high. A few slender pine trees rise tall in the garden. The uncut grass adds to the feeling of unusual peace.

Like the garden, the monastery itself is remote looking, clothed in a deep quiet. Along bare corridors leading to rows of cells on the second floor, sunshine admitted through narrow windows illuminates only a portion of the stone stairway. The walls are whitewashed, and decorated simply with a gray border at the height of a man's shoulder. There are ten cells along the one corridor, five on one side and five on the other. The low and narrow doors are usually left open. But cell number one is shut, and so is cell number five. Padre Pio used to occupy the latter and has only recently moved to cell number one, closer to a terrace which overlooks the garden. The cells stand silent within a deeper silence. Those on the courtyard side are so dark a light is left burning during the day.

In each cell are a small bed, a washstand, a small chest of drawers, a little table with a hardback chair—only the barest necessities. A man who spends a lifetime within these walls demands little in the way of comfort. There is no heat whatever for winter. Five cells have windows over the garden wall, a view of hills and plains, flower bushes with donkey roses.

There are not many birds in San Giovanni Rotondo, except for an occasional passing mountain eagle and a few sparrows in the garden. There are no farms on the mountain. Wandering homeless dogs inhabit isolated haunts, and at night their mournful barking shatters the still air.

Years ago it was possible to sit in the garden with Padre Pio and talk, but today, because of the many hours he spends in the confessional, his day is short. Padre Pio spends but little time in his cell, where he has never accepted any comfort. "I am a *contadino* and have always sat on wooden chairs," he said once to an English lady who was offering him a deep armchair. Similarly he refuses a brazier or gas burner for the cold winter nights. "What would the Holy Father Francis [Saint Francis of Assisi] say about one of his sons with a coal stove in his cell?" he asks.

His gray-painted door is scribbled with names, messages, dates in all the languages of Europe and other continents. The

messages are simple, words of gratitude or hope, faith or piety.
They are cut in with penknives, and overlap one another so
that most of the faded words are unreadable. Corridors and
walls throughout the whole monastery bear messages to him.
When the messages are no longer useful because they cannot
be read, the monks set to work by candlelight with water
buckets and sponges and wipe them all out in the night, wall
by wall, door by door. Then they renew the walls with whitewash. They work so night after night until eventually they
come to Padre Pio's door. Here they halt. They have never
wiped his door clean, and the messages on it bear dates of long
ago. This specific house cleaning is done periodically. The
walls of the *clausura*, long cracked and never repaired, hold
almost as many messages as Padre Pio's door.

Padre Pio leaves the confessional with a hundred confessions
stored in his mind. He makes his way slowly through the
crowded church, slightly wobbling on his wounded feet. Un-
failingly, after he has left the confessional box, he passes
through the *clausura*. Here, beneath the arched ceilings, two
lines of close-shaven men, black-clad and somber looking in
their Sunday best, wait for him.

At noontime there is silence and the men kneel because
Padre Pio is coming. He carries his hands at the level of his
lower ribs, the fingertips touching. His face holds a marked
expression of inward reflection, a look of abstraction and pain.
Ahead of him a monk, walking backwards, takes messages and
donations for Padre Pio. Men put stuffed and sealed envelopes
into his hands. Padre Pio walks slowly, gazing down tenderly

at the upturned faces. His smiling eyes, vivid and steady, seem at the same time utterly untroubled and yet inwardly grieved. And then of a sudden his eyes are nothing but peaceful. His face, round and full with the white curly beard and high, wide forehead, is handsome. Softly he goes on. Then he has passed already and the men watch his cowl. In a second he vanishes through a doorway. The monk who has preceded him closes the door gently, and Padre Pio is out of sight.

Over the door of his cell hangs a sign printed in black ink: "The glory of the world has always sadness for a companion." Here in his cell, at noontime, Padre Pio replaces the blood-soaked linen which covers the wound above his fifth rib. This linen is thick, folded three times over, and it is nine inches wide, entirely covering a wound of two and a half inches.

Padre Pio never uses the hospital. Rather he attends to his wounds himself, and when he has changed the bandages he returns to the friars for his only meal of the day. He eats nothing but vegetables, and drinks only a glass of lemon juice.

Men wait for him in the *clausura* because he will pass again, on his way back to the confessional. The women, left out as it were because they are not allowed to enter the enclosure, crowd the door, gesturing to their men to write a message on the wall for them.

The doorman-Brother, an energetic young man with an intelligent-looking, full-bearded face, hurries to the women. "Please," he begs them, "you are absolutely not allowed in here. Please close this door. It was this draft that gave Padre Pio that bad cold. Please let us keep this door closed because this draft is very dangerous." The women stand back for a few moments, but soon step onto the threshold again, pressing against one another, looking in expectantly.

The doorman-Brother has gone to his counter-window on the ground-floor corridor, and he is busy delivering religious objects wrapped in transparent paper. On each package is written the name of the person for whom it is intended. "This is yours," he is saying, reading the name and then gently handing the package to its owner. Then he hurries back to the women. "But good women, this draft may give him pneumonia. Step back, step back."

The women look at him and then lower their eyes. But they do not move from the *clausura* threshold because Padre Pio is now about to enter the room.

Because people feel that they are important in the heart of Padre Pio, they take the whole monastery, except the cells, to be part of their own realm. They go about as though they were at home, approaching the Brothers at any time. Padre Pio is alone only in the heart of night, when he prays in the choir.

He rises to say Mass at six o'clock in the morning. Now, at seventy-three, he concentrates his full attention on Mass, confession, baptism, first communion, and the marriage ceremony. Years ago he used to hold private meetings and answer his own correspondence with long detailed letters. Today he can answer personally only urgent messages, leaving thousands of letters which come to him daily to be answered by another Brother in his behalf. However, pilgrims feel that Padre Pio has the ability to satisfy the individual while he gives himself to the large group. Only a man who thinks and prays for others as intensely as Padre Pio does can convey such a feeling.

The faithful settle down in San Giovanni Rotondo for days and even weeks, and when utter darkness falls over the hills and the wide road is barely visible in the lights from the hospital, pilgrims still linger about the grounds, often pausing beneath Padre Pio's window. A solitary light shines there, in cell number one. It is two o'clock and Padre Pio has arisen for the *mattutino*, the time when all the Brothers gather for the first time during the day. His moving shadow is visible on the grass, as Padre Pio passes between the window and the light bulb. Pilgrims turn their faces up, straining to hear his foot-steps on the cement floor of the cell, but they are standing twenty feet outside the garden wall and can hear nothing.

Padre Pio has been living here since 1918. In those early days his Mass used to last three hours. His Mass is shorter now. His main mission, the confessional, holds him usually until evening and often until late at night. When fatigue overtakes him he does nothing about it.

As the faithful stand beneath the window at two o'clock in the morning, cars still drive up. Automobiles with plates of all countries in Europe arrive, and Vespas and motor-scooters bring lone pilgrims. Hand in hand, like a brotherhood of hope, people from towns and villages and hamlets all over Italy make the gentle climb to the elm tree and, after parking, back down to the hotels. Once in their rooms people close the window shutters in an attempt to shut out the barking of the dogs.

In just a few hours they will rise, while the moon and stars are still bright. Italian and Spanish and French and English pilgrims will begin to crowd the clearing as the top of the mountain slowly becomes visible and the Lombardy poplars rustle their quivering leaves. There is an air of purity, something from the mountains' earth and the sky, a spiritual texture in the air like the fiber of a soul.

Now and then a voice is heard from courtyards along the road. A mother calls her son, a friend calls a friend, the single voices sounding clear in the mountain silence. Then the voices quickly fade.

The pilgrims who have been watching the light in cell number one now join the faithful in the clearing and the crowd begins to enter Saint Mary of the Graces for Mass.

Soon after Mass, long lines form in front and to the sides of the confessional box. Men and women kneel in the church, where now bright sunshine gleams cheerfully on the spotless floor. Men and women keep their heads lowered in fervent prayer.

Not long ago the police were needed to keep order, but nowadays each person gets a number and accordingly stands in line to go next up to the confessional box. On Sunday, which is the busiest day, Saint Mary of the Graces is packed solid, leaving no room for any chairs. Only five feet of space is left free all around the confessional box, which is new and of light brown, almost blond, wood, with lighter veins running through the surface. On Easter and on Christmas the police are still needed to direct traffic in the clearing.

The Superior, Brother Carmelo da Sessano, and the other eight monks, help Padre Pio with the taxing duties of his extraordinary mission.

Brother Carmelo is forty-five years old, keen and quick. He is a man of great energy. On such occasions as Easter and Christmas, when hundreds of people will detain a Brother with requests for special favors and services, Brother Carmelo watches over his monks. By long experience he is well trained to deal with large and fervent groups, and he has a rare ability to sense when a given situation can grow dangerous. Brother Carmelo never relaxes. Padre Pio is protected from the merely curious and from fanatics. The church and monastery are protected from people looking for relics.

People with cameras, both casual sightseers and professional journalists, seek the intimate and make impossible requests. Patiently, the monks stop them.

"I'd like to take a picture for my newspaper while he changes the linen on his wounds."

"You cannot."

"But it shows the people the side wound."

"I am sorry."

From this moment on the photographer is not allowed into the monastery. There are several photographs of Padre Pio in existence. Those taken during the Mass, when his hands are free of their customary half-gloves, reveal the wounds in his palms clearly. The Brothers have no objection to such pictures. They merely forbid the intimate glimpses requested by sensation hunters.

As for entering the door which leads to the corridor on the second story, where the cells are located, the doorman-Brother permits such a privilege only when he is sure the visitor can be fully trusted. Over the years hundreds of people have been

trusted. Over the years thousands of people have never disappointed the Brothers. On Padre Pio's door, their messages
still stand.

Among the people allowed to enter that particular corridor
are priests, often high officials of the Church, whose faces
glow as they approach cell number one. Many priests request
the privilege of serving at the Mass of Padre Pio.

In winter the pilgrims make their way up to the monastery
with shovels, laboriously clearing a path. No hardship stops
them from arriving punctually for Mass.

The Mass is now not so long as it was in years past, yet in its
spiritual quality it is much the same as in the olden days. As
Padre Pio goes into ecstasy, he becomes a spectacle of agony.
His eyes are shut, his face contorted in pain, his lips trembling,
his cheeks wet with tears. His ecstasy lasts long while he re-
lives the Passion of the Cross. For several minutes he leans on
the altar and weeps, standing perfectly still in mystical trans-
port. The expression on his face is that of a nomad of the beyond.

This is the man believers say is a saint and makes miracles.

Chapter 2

ORAZIO FORGIONE and his wife, Maria Giuseppe De Nunzio Forgione, both of Pietrelcina, registered the birth of Francesco at nine o'clock in the morning on May 26, 1887. The registration took place in the City Hall, in the presence of the mayor and the village assessor, Signor Gaetano Sagliocco. The father and the mother, twenty-six and twenty-eight years old, gave their address as Vico Storto, number 25. The child was born, they said, on May 25, 1887.

Witnesses to the registration were a shoemaker, Luciano Pennisi, and a man who owned a plot of land, Don Antonio De Michele. Francesco was baptized on the same day, with the midwife, Grazia Formichelli, of Pietrelcina, acting as godmother.

Pietrelcina in those days was a mountain town of three thousand people. Like all the other hamlets around Campobasso and Benevento and Avellino, it had only one noteworthy feature, and that was its poverty. Its only connection with the outside world was a donkey and mule trail from Benevento, a trail lost in the hills to the north at the level of Campobasso. It was remote, both from the cities of Italy and from the two seas siding the peninsula. Pietrelcina's poor were well ac-

quainted with hunger and sickness and death. The hamlet has
grown so slowly that in 1959 it registered no more than six
thousand inhabitants.

Orazio and Maria Giuseppe were among the more fortunate
families of the village, for they had a little plot of land to
farm. They shared it with a relative who was too old to take
care of it himself and who, wishing to help the Forgione
family, had put what he owned into their hands. The old
relative shared in the harvest, but he also helped pay the taxes
on the property.

The years following Francesco's birth were hard ones for
the Forgiones. Every day, except in winter, Orazio and Maria
Giuseppe started to work at sunup and returned to Vico Storto
at sundown, Orazio riding a donkey, the wife walking behind
balancing on her head a basket containing the vegetables, the
wine, the bread saved from their lunch. In winter they worked
at mending the tools they used for the farm work. The work
was disheartening, for most of the tools were too far gone to
mend.

If Orazio could save, say in five, six, or even ten years, a
few lire each harvest time, then he could pay for a passport and
a boat ticket, and have enough left over to buy a meal in New
York before joining the caravans of foreign labor building a
railroad on the west shore of the Hudson River.

America. But how far it was! Even Naples seemed endless
miles away. Rome sounded like a city in another country—
and yet, somehow, Rome was able to collect taxes. To be sure,
taxes were but a few lire, but then again, the price of a donkey

was a few lire. So perhaps Rome was not so far away after all. And if Rome was not so far away, maybe even America was within reach.

While the Forgiones saved their lire and dreamed of America, starvation and sickness and death haunted Vico Storto. Little time elapsed between Francesco's birth and the arrival of a little sister. Orazio and Maria Giuseppe then had four little ones—Felicia, Michele, Francesco, and Grazia—to house and clothe and feed. The family's little plot of land did not quite support them. Moreover, Orazio, illiterate himself, wanted his sons and daughters to learn how to read and write. But he could not feed them and send them to school too. Only if he went to America would that be possible.

If he went to America, he would be able to mail them a part of his good wages. Then up and down Vico Storto, as in all Pietrelcina, hunger could dance its terrifying dance, but his wife and children would have food, and there would be money for the children's schooling.

Was there money to be earned in the next village? No. In the nearest city? No. Money could be earned only far away: in America. So on winter nights Orazio's companions, coming to talk by the meager fire of twigs, tried to help him figure out how many lire he would have to save to go to America. After every few words, the name of God was mentioned. On the naked floor the four children huddled about the fire away from the cold. Francesco always sat close to his father, attentive, often lifting his glance at the talk.

Orazio's companions asked, "Why does he look up when we mention Christ?"

"Who knows," Orazio answered. "He just looks up, poor little Christian."

And Maria Giuseppe would say, "It is because I remind you not to mention God's name in vain."

"That must be the reason," agreed Orazio.

In those days even large cities like Naples had but few gas lamps. On the long winter nights Pietrelcina, half buried in the snow, lay clothed in darkness. Wolves howled beneath the windows. In spring, when the snow melted, it was like Venice. Water lapped at the front doors of the little houses. Floods, carrying stones and mud, rose knee-deep in the streets, and the people lived in a state of emergency, with few supplies. Three thousand people were crowded in a land that could barely support three hundred. Only three families were well off.

"Us poor Christians," said Orazio's companions. "We are truly poor. Who knows why?"

In summer in the fields, Orazio's companions would repeat what had been said all winter. Words, once uttered, were never forgotten in Pietrelcina. Poor as the South was, it was a land rich in memories. Not only every word, but the accent too, the tone with which a word was spoken, was learned by heart.

Orazio never thought of taking his family to America. The Erie Railroad job was man's work. He was going to work and would return home from the job. The plan involved an odd sort of commuting. He liked to think he was not leaving home. Like other *contadini* elsewhere in Italy, he believed that farming was a way of life, as natural as breathing. Railroad labor in America was a measure required in an emergency, a necessity that befell poor people in dire need of quick money.

In the fields and at home Orazio would often find Francesco's eyes turned to him, the child's florid face smiling.

"He looks at me all the time. I wonder why."

"This child loves you dearly, and there is always this talk about the Erie Railroad. So it is as if you were leaving us ten times a day for Naples," Maria Giuseppe said. "When you go out I see his eyes follow you. It seems Franci wants to say something to you. You have noticed?"

"I have," he said. "But the other children do not keep on watching me, though they also love me. But let him. I like it, poor little Christian."

"There is love and great love," concluded Maria Giuseppe. These words, like so many others, were stored in the memory of the town. In the South, remembering everything was a way of life.

Spain's domination had left its marks on Pietrelcina. The language included many Spanish words, and the people wore Spanish styles of clothing. In their food, they used olive oil heavily, in the Spanish manner. Moorish tunes in songs were part of their inheritance. And so, when they gathered around the priest, Don Salvatore Pannullo, they did so the Italian way with familiarity and ease, but also with Spanish dignity. They would bring their children to him and he would say, "Young plants need a lot of care."

There was Francesco, close to his father and smiling at the priest.

"Franci has this sweet smile. My other children should be as friendly," said Orazio.

Don Salvatore said, "It is good. It is a sign that he has known kindness."

"Kindness solves the problems of the world," said Orazio.

And the priest nodded. "You have a good heart."

Don Salvatore was the archpriest of Pietrelcina, but it was not he who kept school. A man named Domenico Tezzani, who had studied for the priesthood but left the seminary before being ordained, was the schoolmaster. Soon Francesco would be his pupil. At the sight of Tezzani little Francesco would grip his father's hand and hold it tightly. His smile would vanish. His distress was so pronounced that Orazio worried about it, and would say to Maria Giuseppe, "I wish the archpriest were the teacher, for I am afraid Franci will not do well in school because of Tezzani. Why does he not like him?"

They sat on the doorstep, with the neighbors, early in the evening.

"Who likes him? He said he was going to be a priest and he studied to be a priest. But when it came time to be a priest, he said he wasn't going to be. Now, what is he? Expriest," answered Maria Giuseppe.

At this time the Forgione's aging relative, who had owned property of his own in addition to the little plot they were farming, decided to give them the larger farm as well. It was not far from Pietrelcina. On the land stood a farmhouse of three rooms, which was a decided asset. With a house on the farm itself, they could stay on the land when the weather was bad, and avoid the trip to Vico Storto.

With the larger farm, the family's work increased. They expected their income to increase too, but at harvest time they realized that their condition would not change. The only good thing about the new farm was its house. The land itself was poor. The one tool, *la zappa*, bit into dust. When Orazio drove it deeper, all day long he uncovered stones that made the *zappa* sparkle.

"The *zappa* should be the flag of Italy," Orazio used to say.

With the help of *la zappa* they managed to raise a straggling crop of grain. Then, Spanish style, they stood in the clearing with pitchforks, lifting straw into the breeze to separate stalk from grain. They sweated their garments and the sweat dried on them and they sweated over again and drank water. Little Francesco was too young to help with the work, but all day long he kept shuttling to and from the well, carrying pails of water for the workers, until finally the sun went down.

A meager supper. Darkness. Silence in the countryside. At midnight, a sudden storm, lightning, rain, wind. A terrifying rumble of big rocks. In the morning, all around stood men wearing rags, naked children, women in disheveled nightdresses. Downhill, the houses were all flooded. The survivors wept with abandon.

In Pietrelcina the storm had done even worse damage. Donkeys and goats and pigs, men and women and children had sought refuge in the piazza, away from the narrow, dangerous streets and lanes. There they huddled, like a defeated army in a last ditch. But this kind of battle was never over, and to-morrow it would begin again.

Little Francesco was trotting after his father down the field. On the stony path rested an old man, chest caved in, face brutalized with unrewarding labors. At the feet of the old man was a little girl, with sores all over her face.

"*Tata!*" Francesco cried.

"What?" said Orazio, turning to his son.

"Look."

The old man, the little girl.

Orazio stepped closer and leaned down. The old man was dead.

"Do not look, do not look," said Orazio. "Do not look at the face of death, you are too young."

But Francesco stared at the stilled face, upon which flies began to gather. Orazio called for help. He shouted up and down the path, into the open empty country. Echoes responded, then silence. "These poor Christians. Go call your mother. Run quick, Franci." Gently he lifted the little girl in his arms.

And another day, on the same path, a donkey stopped. The owner pulled hard on the hemp rope, but the donkey would not budge. The man picked up a log and beat the donkey on the head until the animal curled his legs, then rolled over on his side.

Again, "*Tata! Tata!*"

"Oh, Lord," said Orazio.

Francesco began to look sick. His once florid cheeks grew white, and then sunken. Over and over, he would call, "Daddy, Daddy." Against all pain, his cries turned to his father. Orazio never failed to answer, and yet the boy wept on the sorrows around him, and called and wept until his voice was nothing but a murmur of heavy sadness.

"Why do you cry?" asked the mother.

But Orazio answered, "What his eyes see is no laughing matter."

And Francesco still saw the sored face of the little girl, and the flies on the old man's eyelids. He was no longer a mere child.

Out on the land with other farmers, Orazio tried to explain why his son looked ill. "Franci is not like my other children, who play with our dog and are just children. Franci has the gift of loving people and is making a personal sickness out of their misfortunes. It is Pietrelcina that is making him ill."

And the other farmers nodded sadly.

"Do you think conditions will ever change here?" Orazio asked.

In those days Italy's premier was Giovanni Giolitti, educated in Turin in the North, and risen to premier after several minor public jobs. Under his administration, universal suffrage had been introduced. His government, the same parliament that

saw Garibaldi seated as deputy, expanded colonial policies in
Tripoli. Money went into the burden of colonies, and
Pietrelcina was left without a cent.

At six, Francesco already seemed overwhelmed at the many
and various sorrows he had seen. The archpriest Don Salvatore,
a distant relative of the Forgione's, worried about the boy who
mused so sorrowfully upon sorrow. When he played, his
mother told the priest, he did not play as other children did.
Often, with an expression of deep compassion on his face, he
would join twigs and sticks in the shape of the cross. Don
Salvatore began to watch Francesco more closely than ever.
What with weeding and sowing and harvesting, and the
laborious cleaning and washing and cooking done in the primitive rooms of Vico Storto, mothers had little time for their
children. The archpriest would gather the youngsters around
him and take them out for walks.

Don Salvatore called them his *chierichetti*, his dear little
ones, and he used to say that some would surely become priests
one day. They trotted after his soutane, Francesco the young-
est of the lot. He would lead them a little way below the
church of Santa Maria Degli Angeli, along a country path
loud with crowing roosters.

On such a little walk one day, Don Salvatore heard the
children laughing more than usual. He turned, and said,
"What is it?"

Francesco said. "I said I heard bells ringing loudly, and they
are laughing because they do not hear them. But I did hear
them, really I did."

"What bells?"

"Church bells. Right here, I think a great church will be built."

"A great church? Right here?"

"Yes, a great church will be built here."

Don Salvatore, as all the people of Pietrelcina would, remembered those words. But he made no comment to Francesco. Instead, he said, "Let us turn around," and he led the children back to the tortuous streets of Pietrelcina. He went straight to Maria Giuseppe, and said, "Maria Giuse, I cannot truly say I understand Franci very well."

"Who understands Franci?" said Maria Giuseppe. "He sits and builds a cross with sticks. I say to the women at the fountain that Franci is your best *chierichetto*."

"Yes, he is my best *chierichetto*," said the archpriest, and he continued on his way home.

The Forgione children were growing up, and still it was all their overburdened parents could do to feed their family. To educate them—ah, that would take money from America. One day, Orazio packed his satchel and put it under the bed. By this means, he hoped to make Maria Giuseppe feel the imminence of his departure, and grieve over his absence while he was still there to comfort her. Maria Giuseppe did not weep, but she left the care of donkey, chicken, pigs, and goats and went to lament in the rectory. "Soon I will be left all alone." She stood facing the kindly archpriest. Maria Giuseppe was a small woman, bony, dark-skinned, black-haired, with a deep line between her eyebrows, other lines at the sides of her mouth, her lips dry from the open air of the fields. Her face revealed determination and force and all the pressing realities of labors, and little else. "I'll be left all alone, and let me tell you what Franci said to me when I told him. He asked, how far is the monastery for the poor monks."

"Poor monks?"

"He wants to become a monk."

Don Salvatore thought it significant that the wish should have been expressed as soon as the mother had informed him that his father had finally decided to depart now by selling a portion of the farm, rather than sometime later when he might have saved enough lire. The boy was probably wishing to replace his father with Our Father, said the priest.

Weeks passed, and every Sunday, Maria Giuseppe took the satchel out from under the bed, dusted it carefully, and replaced it under the bed. Still she did not weep. She was too busy with her children, too determined to better her lot with the money from America.

One day before the end of summer, when Francesco was seven years old, Orazio began to make the rounds, shaking hands from house to house and from farm to farm. Then the whole family dressed in their Sunday best. Orazio's companions came to help carry the satchel to the piazza. There a cart waited, to take him to Naples and the ship. A number of women gave him letters for their husbands in America. In tears, Orazio kissed his children and shook hands formally with Maria Giuseppe.

Francesco said, "I pray for you."

Orazio had not expected those words as a farewell, and he

paused and looked at the boy with an expression of wonder. And he was deeply moved.

When the cart drove off, Maria Giuseppe gathered her children at her skirt, her hands moving from head to head. Her eyes filled with tears. There was Orazio already in the distance, standing up and balancing himself on the wobbly cart, waving.

Maria Giuseppe returned to the empty rooms and shut the door. She did not howl and tear her hair and beat her head against the wall. At the fountain in the morning her neighbors asked her why she had been so quiet. "I respect my children's feelings. I would not frighten them that way. It is enough that they have lost the father. Should they also see that the mother has gone to pieces?"

School in those days cost a sack of grain and five lire a year, twelve cents in American money for the four children. Maria Giuseppe could well afford to pay, now that Orazio sent her a large portion of his earnings each month.

But Tezzani stopped at the public fountain to talk to her, shaking his head. "Listen. You have no money troubles, of course, but there are other difficulties, I am sorry to say. Franci is good only to watch the goats. Put a *zappa* on his shoulder, and you will see, he will be a happy farmer."

"*Signor Maestro*, how can I let the archpriest, who writes the letters for me, write this to my husband?"

The teacher complained to Don Salvatore, too, that Francesco was not a good student. After all the sacrifices Orazio had made, paying for the passport, the ride to Naples, the overnight stay in Naples, the boat ticket, so that he could earn money to pay for Francesco's education, Francesco did not care to be educated. Don Salvatore heard Tezzani out in silence. Then he called Maria Giuseppe to the church.

"The teacher is not pleased."

"My son has intelligence to sell. So then, what is wrong?" Her voice sounded as strong as her face looked.

"He longs for his father, and perhaps it is this longing that distracts him. And it is mixed up with church bells he hears, and the great church that he thinks will be built in Pietrelcina. He needs, wants his father."

"I am here." A matriarchal determination was part of her nature.

At seven, Francesco Forgione knelt in the straw hut next to the house on the farm, praying that the Lord should take care of his father.

He had turned his eyes up to his father, and now that his father was in America, he was turning his eyes up to the light which filtered through the straw.

Soon he stopped murmuring, "Lord, take care of me, my Daddy is away," and prayed only for others, the suffering people of his native town.

He prayed that God should take care of the little girl whose face was festered, and the soul of her grandfather who died on the path. He prayed for the children the floods had carried off, and asked forgiveness for the man who had killed the donkey.

People with eleven fingers, hunchbacks, deaf mutes, and a

score of blind populated the twisted alleys of Pietrelcina. These Francesco included in the realm of suffering. Foreign winds met and clashed, the *scirocco* from Africa, the *bora* from the Adriatic, the *tramontana*, a wind rising at sundown from the Tyrrhenian Sea. These winds climbed the long chain of hills which run the length of the peninsula, bringing up germs from the plains, the malaria of the flat lands. Here the width of the peninsula is only seventy miles from sea to sea, and over half of those miles are made of mountains. All too often, in those days, death was the only outsider to penetrate the isolation of the hill country. Francesco included all the poor, suffering farmers of the region in his prayers.

Too, he prayed that he should do well in school. To his teacher, Tezzani, he was still the student who showed no promise. Signor Tezzani returned to complain to his mother periodically, but she refused to write such news to her husband in America and remained firm in her belief that something was wrong with the teacher, not the student. She begged the archpriest to find another teacher for Francesco.

Don Salvatore considered the request seriously, despite the shortage of schools and teachers in the area. While the apostolic jurisdiction of Milan had seven hundred parochial schools, the South, with the island of Sicily included, had only five for each diocese. Schools were therefore crowded. Among the nineteen diocesan regions, gathering thirty-nine apostolic provinces, that of the Benevento diocese, with seventy illiterates for each one hundred persons, was among the most desperately in need of schools.

Nevertheless, Maria Giuseppe continued to press the arch-

priest, and when she had the next letter written for her, she
happily announced to Orazio that Francesco had found another teacher, Don Angelo Caccavo. Suddenly, Francesco
changed from a poor pupil to a brilliant one.

Francesco still did not take part in the games of children
his age. He spent most of his time in the straw hut next door
to the farmhouse. But when the time came for examinations for
the fourth and last year of grammar school, he not only passed,
but received grades of ninety and a hundred. He was now
ready for his first Latin lessons.

The following year Orazio returned. It was common for
Italians who worked in America to spend their savings visiting
their wives and children in Italy every year. In a lifetime of
work in America, men like Orazio would return for a brief
visit as often as twenty times.

Orazio, at his first return trip, found his family lifted from
the bottom of the tragic financial scale, thanks to his salary of
nine dollars a week. With the change in his pocket, he bought
Francesco his first Latin grammar.

Maria Giuseppe wept with joy. She gave a feast for all of
Orazio's companions.

Francesco was nine years old, and a serious, grown-up
child. "Son," Orazio asked, "have you thought of what you
want to be when you are older?"

"I want to be a monk."

"Eh?" Orazio would raise his left eyebrow. "Very well, if
you show such inclination and do well in school, I will make

a monk out of you. Not a beggar monk. I will not have you a beggar, because at times the monks who beg are welcomed when they knock, but often the door is shut on their faces, and often people turn their dogs loose."

Accordingly, Francesco would go to the theological academy. He would be a monk, yes, but a monk educated and ordained a priest and officially permitted therefore to say Mass. In the language of the Forgiones and the people feasting in the house, he would be *monaco da Messa*.

This meant Orazio would have to make sure to return to America and arrive on the day he told his foreman he would be there. But he would go with high spirits and a hopeful heart. In the South, as elsewhere in Italy, the education of a young man in the higher Catholic schools brought prestige to his family. His son Michele would have a brother in the seminary, Felicia and Grazia, his daughters, would belong to the circle of those girls who had a brother in the seminary. The light would reflect on him and his wife.

Maria Giuseppe was happy. Only the sons of landowners who would spend the winters in Naples, the sons of big *possidenti*, could afford to go to school. Francesco's wish was even better. It was a greater honor.

But the school boys reacted differently. The boys who felt a liking for Francesco supported him and expressed their pride, but others turned their backs maliciously. *"Lu monaco,"* they said in Neapolitan dialect, the inflection implying oddity, and sounding at the same time like awe. They could not help wondering what went on within him. In the long summer eve-

nings, in the piazza of upper Pietrelcina, around the church of
Saint Pius V, they commented enviously on his character. "He
never did belong. He was born a monk."

The town heard what Don Angelo Caccavo said to his
mother. "I do not know what else to teach your son. This boy
knows more than I do already." And the mothers and fathers
turned to their sons, "You should be like Francesco Forgione.
Look at Franci. You are a *scugnizzo* and Franci is a true
scholar. Already he knows more than Don Angelo and Don
Angelo said so himself."

In their defense the boys answered, "Franci calls himself a
macaroni without salt. He can't run, can't jump, can't climb
trees. He says himself that he is good for nothing, a macaroni
without salt."

Francesco's judgment of himself baffled Pietrelcina, and the
archpriest answered the people, "Nobody knows what will
become of Francesco."

His voice had a tone of wonder, because, when Francesco
was just nine years old, his mother had found him sleeping in
the straw hut for the night. She had informed the archpriest
that Francesco did not wish to sleep in his bed, but stretched
out on the naked floor of the hut.

Francesco was not afraid to sleep in the hut through the
long night, while all the dogs barked. He was not afraid to be
alone. He was not afraid to face the earth and the universe on
his own two feet, of this Don Salvatore was sure. The kindly
archpriest had learned while questioning him that Francesco
simply did not know what fear was.

·"He feels free," Don Salvatore said to Maria Giuseppe.

"Free?"

"Is not bound by fear." The archpriest had noticed that Francesco would often say, to his mother, his brother, his sisters and his cousins, "Do not fear. What should you be afraid of?" This courage of Francesco's made the archpriest see in a sharper light that others were constantly frightened, while the boy was not.

Don Salvatore had so far perceived three qualities which Francesco possessed strongly: intelligence, sensitivity to the suffering around him, and courage. It seemed to him that Francesco's courage had a mystical quality, because of the serenity with which Francesco imparted it to others. The good country priest knew the implications, the possibilities contained in any power, so that he began to think of guiding Francesco where he wished to be guided, into the monastery. Indeed, Pietrelcina needed a great deal of everything, but most of all it needed prayers.

Francesco prayed repeatedly the evening long in the little hut. Then, exhausted, he would not have the strength to walk from the hut to the house, and would simply curl up on the floor and close his eyes.

But it was very important that he should sleep in bed, because if other boys learned what Francesco was doing, they would make fun of him. The kind of teasing that went on in Pietrelcina was not the usual, innocent fun of boys. The isolation of the little community gave life there special conditions, and among children, subtle but disastrous battles went on. The battles could have lasting effects, especially to a sensitive boy.

Adults simply thought, "They are playing," while the victim was cruelly persecuted.

Don Salvatore talked to Francesco in his delicate, deeply benevolent way. "What is the matter, you do not like your bed, Franci?"

The Forgiones, and Don Salvatore with them, wished to keep Francesco's intense prayers and his habit of sleeping in the hut a secret, so Michele, Felicia, and Grazia never spoke of their brother to the other boys. Maria Giuseppe began to hold her tongue when she met other women at the fountain.

When he was not praying in the hut, Francesco took solitary walks up the mountain, along empty trails. The boy climbed slowly, with his head lifted to the top of the hills and the sky. He wore a black suit of homespun wool and a white shirt without collar and tie. On the top of the mountain, he would sit and rest and watch the town, his face intent and perfectly quiet, as he thought about his plans to leave home. He watched women tending goats on the edges of the lonely trails—black-clad women, their black kerchiefs binding head and face, except the eyes, against dust. While they minded the animals, the women all worked at their knitting. Francesco would stay long up the mountain, and then slowly return home.

Talking to the archpriest about how monastery life would be, he looked confident and sure of himself. There were several monasteries in the region, and even a few abbeys. Still, their number was not high compared with the many churches —three or four to every town in the four regions of Benevento, Avellino, Naples, and Salerno. Most of the monks inhabiting the convents came from other regions, from Umbria and Abruzzi and Tuscany and elsewhere. For Neapolitans, a friar of their own region was a rare, rather than a common sight. Traditionally, parents would encourage their sons to enter seminaries, not monasteries. So Don Salvatore thought Francesco's decision to become an exception was in itself in the realm of courage. It was sad for him to visualize the boy's going to live in some remote location in the mountains of the Apennine or the hills of the Cilento, or somewhere on the narrow plains around the gulfs, in the climate of the sea.

"You will have a longing for home," murmured the archpriest, "our home, whatever it is."

"Yes, I know I will miss it," Francesco answered. His home was very simple, the rooms bare of comfort: a kitchen wall blackened by chimney smoke, primitive wooden chairs, enormous solid-wood beds high from the floor where produce of the land was stored. At supper time the family sat two feet away from the table, reaching out for the food poured in one main dish placed in the middle of the table. The children slept in cold rooms in the winter, and before they went to bed Maria Giuseppe warmed a brick by the fire, wrapped it in woolens and put it at the foot of the bed. If any of the children was ill, she filled a closed brazier with embers and ironed the sheet with the bottom of the brazier.

Francesco would not have had his home any other way. He belonged to the peasant people, and, no matter what the future would bring, he would not budge from them. The food of his home was bread and onions, bread and wine, bread and

olive oil and garlic. They rarely had any meat to eat, and fish
was never used. But Maria Giuseppe would brew chicken
broth when any of the children were sick. On religious holi-
days she would have tender goats, lamb, pasta stuffed with
ricotta. The very simplicity and utter cleanliness of the foods
and garments made of their poverty a wholesome and dignified condition. True, their dishes were wooden, but the
wood was good. The rooms were bare, but the walls lasted a
thousand years. The floors were naked, but in width and
thickness the flagstones were priceless. There was only whitewash instead of paint, but the house, bathed in sunrise and
sundown, gleamed like snow.

The poverty of the people in the South was, just at that
time, only one of the burdens Italy had to bear. The country
was still mourning the assassination of King Humbert I, the
good King who had left his Royal Palace in Rome to help the
people of Naples during the plague of 1884. They had called
him *Umberto il buono*, the good Humbert. Misfortunes and
economic crises had played havoc with his brief reign. With
the occupation of Massaua, in Africa, in 1885, Italy had
founded its overseas territory. War with Ethiopia seemed in-
evitable. In the near future, people not leaving for America
would be fighting at Adua, in Africa.

Francesco's road was quite different: a twisted narrow
mountain path up to one of the nearby monasteries, isolation
and silence and meditation and prayer.

Francesco had lived so far by himself, for the intensity of
his prayer was all the company he needed. Going to school
and back, in the hut near the farmhouse, in the empty rooms

of Vico Storto, always, he was alone. But now he found himself the center of attention. As Maria Giuseppe, who had
tended to the satchel for Orazio's long sea trip, prepared
Francesco's valise for a trip seemingly much farther than beyond the seas, the neighborhood women gathered round. She
who had always made all the clothes for the family herself,
now asked one of the seamstresses to prepare a *corredo* for
Francesco. On the fingers of both hands she counted all the
pieces of the *corredo* she put in the valise, woolen underwear
and calico shirts and the socks knitted by the women on the
trails, the goat tenders. The evening before Francesco's departure, she closed the valise for the night. In the morning she
opened it to add one last provision, a piece of bread fresh from
the oven.

The archpriest was to accompany Francesco part of the
way out of town. In the house on Vico Storto, neighborhood
women clustered around the boy. To the proud, saddened
mother, they murmured, "Blessed is the house which has a
tonsure." In a few days Francesco's hair would be cut circu-
larly, shaved on top.

Maria Giuseppe began to weep. Her son Michele and her
daughters tried to comfort her, but try as she would, she
could not control her sorrow. How she would have liked to
have her husband to support her this day!

The archpriest whispered to his young protégé, "Franci,
you are going into secluded meditation. Promise me you will
not completely forget and abandon your body for your soul.
Even the most devout monk, who needs so little, needs his
strength."

Relatives and friends came to the house to say good-by,

and Francesco was suddenly confused and drew back quietly. He took the valise from his mother's shaking hands and made his way toward the door.

"Courage," Don Salvatore said softly as he watched his favorite of the *chierichetti* set out on his determined path, to his first monastery. Francesco had made the first step toward being a monk-priest.

Chapter 3

Morcone, closer to Campobasso, is still in the Benevento
Province, but it is higher on the Apennines than Pietrelcina.
Today it is a town of ten thousand people, but in 1902, it
numbered only a little over five thousand.

At the time Francesco arrived in Morcone, Italy was busy
renewing the Triple Alliance with Germany and Austria for
the second time. But the humble little town of Morcone was
as far above political alliances and diplomatic intrigues as the
crest of the Apennines was above the flat lands of Mediter-
ranean shores. In October it was colder here, in Morcone,
than in Pietrelcina. The snow on the lofty Apennines was but
a short distance away. Suddenly homesick, Francesco was
torn between his ambition and his sense of responsibility, for
back in Pietrelcina, he had left his home to be managed by the
mother in the absence of the father. The suffering of the
world at large began to recede, and the homesick feeling grew
more and more intense as he approached the monastery.

Francesco had with him a letter from the archpriest. He
paused at the door of the monastery and took the letter out.
There he stood a moment, looking at the lumbering structure
of the monastery, and holding the letter. Who would take the

letter? There was deep silence about, and not a person in sight.

He stood gazing at the monastery door and the monastery walls, walls that loomed in a silence buried in a deeper silence. The monastery seemed vacant. Doors and windows were all closed. He stared at the whitewashed stones. The simplicity of line of the whole structure was as cold as the October day. He glanced at the empty grounds of a garden tucked away in isolation. On the other hand this was what he wanted, and the awesome isolation seemed friendly to him, even sheltering.

A side door gave under the pressure of his hands. He entered, and without pausing at all, climbed a stairway. He found a room, empty, like the garden and the halls. He set down his valise, opened the window, and gazed long toward Pietrelcina.

The monastery was functioning. Friars and priests lived here with a group of novices. But Francesco had not come to be with or without people. He had come to learn how to pray. And he had come to learn what he did not know of the Roman Catholic Church.

The novices, from villages of the South, were preoccupied with the idea of authority. Many of them seemed to have no ambition but to show their respect for the monks and priests who were their spiritual and intellectual teachers. Others, less cowed by the disciplinary aspect of monastery life, worried about their studies and examinations to the point of nightmares. The ones with less intelligence worked twice as hard as the others, determined not to lose face, not only in the eyes of their relatives, but also in the esteem of their whole villages.

The teachers whose presence called forth such anxious feelings were benevolent and wise. The difference in age between teachers and students seemed not twenty years, but endless decades. Even the younger teachers seemed to be very old men.

The oldest students were already closer to the wise old men than to the shallow youth. In just a few years they would themselves be the benevolent and wise teachers. It was as though an hour in the monastery were two hours, a year two years, ten years two decades.

The work of a student in the monastery was laborious. It seemed to be all uphill. Now and then flashes of sheer illumination possessed them all, and in these moments they were happy young men. But always, the skies clouded evenly gray again.

Francesco began to pass the nights on his knees. He would not read the Gospel standing up, for it seemed to him that this posture lacked respect. He read the Gospel on his knees.

For a whole year, he prayed long hours in the night, not caring what was happening to his flesh and bones. He prayed to be recognized by the Poor Man of Assisi as one of his sons.

Francesco's face turned pale, and he lost weight. Night after night he spent on his knees. And now he spat a little blood in his handkerchief.

On January 22, 1903, in the chapel of the Morcone monastery, Francesco Forgione received the brown robe and white sash that were the habit of the Brothers of Saint Francis. For his new name, he chose Frate Pio, in honor of the patron Saint of Pietrelcina, Saint Pio V.

On January 25, when the snow lay deep in the fields around Morcone and the countryside was totally deserted, there was a visitor for Francesco Forgione.

"Who?"

"The boy from my town. I left him here just last year, as I was on my way to Campobasso. I brought him here in my cart."

"You mean Frate Pio."

"I mean Francesco Forgione of Pietrelcina."

"Yes, that is his name now, Frate Pio."

"Since when?"

"Three days ago."

"May I see him?"

Francesco appeared. On seeing him, the cartman was silent for a moment. Then, "You look so tall," he said. "It is because all your flesh is gone. You have reduced yourself to skin and bones."

Frate Pio, like the other young novices, was bound by the rule of silence. The master of novices had granted him permission to speak to the cartman, but the fewer words he said, the better. So he did not respond to the man's observation, but handed him a bundle and said, "Here, take this with you, if you will. My civilian clothes. Tell my mother, tell my brother and my sisters, tell the archpriest that on the twenty-second I received the habit."

"Who knows just when I'll get to Pietrelcina, for I am forced to wait in Morcone until this snow melts. There has been no post to Pietrelcina for a month because of the snow."

But the cartman took the bundle willingly. "Must I tell them also," he added, "that you are skin and bones?"

Frate Pio was silent. They stood a moment longer just inside the main door, the cartman gazing at the walls. The thickness of its walls made the Morcone seminary look like a palace in the castle country of France, only without the towers and drawbridges. The cartman blinked. Then he turned again to Frate Pio. In farewell, all he said was, "Franci, you are very sick."

The Guardian Brother, Father Agostino, had noted Frate Pio's thinness and pallor. Worried, he called the country doctor of Morcone to visit Frate Pio. Frate Pio told them quite calmly that his health had been declining since he was nine years old. The doctor was concerned with his condition, but expressed hope that it might improve and decided to wait a few months before making a definite prognosis.

Before the doctor's second visit, Maria Giuseppe arrived one day in Morcone. She wore her best dress, a simple, gray frock with pleats beneath the small collar. A gray kerchief covered her curly black hair. She was alone when she arrived at the monastery. Patiently, she looked about the silent building for someone to talk to. It was early July and the weather was hot. Finally, in the garden, she met Father Agostino, "father" to the boys, who smilingly said: "Frate Pio does not exist."

"What happened to my son?" cried Maria Giuseppe in alarm. "He is here."

The priest hastily defined the expression he had used, by

which he had meant to praise Frate Pio. "Those who are genuinely good," he explained, "move about in the world without stepping on your toes." Maria Giuseppe's alarm quickly gave way to shy pride in her son.

Father Agostino called Frate Pio.

A little later, in the good shade of the garden, Frate Pio and Maria Giuseppe sat quietly face to face, the mother with a wicker basket on her lap, producing out of it handfuls of home made *paste*, Frate Pio eating slowly, peacefully, and in silence. They gazed tenderly at one another, both faces expressing peaceful contentment. Maria Giuseppe concealed her worries about his health, because she feared that words of sorrow or anxiety would trouble him. But all the way back to Pietrelcina she wept.

When the doctor saw Frate Pio the second time, he was by no means reassured by the boy's condition. A letter for Maria Giuseppe arrived in Pietrelcina. Clutching it, she ran to the archpriest. He read, "We cannot say that his health is truly good, and we would like to have a visit from Signor Orazio Forgione."

In tears, Maria Giuseppe exclaimed, "My husband is coming. He is on the ocean now."

No sooner had Orazio arrived in Pietrelcina than he left again, on his way to Morcone. He would not risk taking a slow mule cart, so he bought a ticket on the train instead. But the train ride was maddening. The train spent more time stopping for water and coal than it did traveling, and the journey took longer for Orazio, on the efficient modern conveyance, than it had taken for his son months before, in a humble cart.

Orazio had all he could do to contain his impatience. Was all his hope and pride in his Franci to be shattered because of illness? Just how sick was the florid boy he had left behind with his wife? Was he, Orazio, in any way to blame for the sickness? Had he not gone to America, had he stayed at home to take care of his family in person, would this have happened? With fear and grief, Orazio approached the looming, whitewashed stone structure of the monastery.

Was the trouble in Franci's lungs? Were there special medicines he could have in America?

The Guardian Brother invited Orazio to sit down in the small waiting room. There, in the shadows, Orazio lowered his head, his calloused hands resting on his knees. He could not bear to gaze at Father Agostino's face. At a first glance, he had understood what that face was saying.

The monk stood silent watching the anguished farmer, who sat perfectly still, as though some motion of his might bring tragedy closer. When Orazio finally looked up, he saw that the friar would have liked to keep his silence unbroken, rather than to hurt him. Then Father Agostino's eyes filled with tears.

"Your son. . . ."

"Please, I want to know," begged Orazio.

"It is incredible. It seems that Frate Pio has not touched food for twenty-one days. Only the Holy Ghost. And now, well, now you see."

Orazio rose, and his hat dropped to his feet. "Twenty-one days?"

"You have to take him home. There is nothing else to do.

You have to take him home with you because he is seriously ill."

"Home?"

The priest waited.

"Home?" Orazio was stunned. "But of course, at once. I will take care of my son."

"We have done all we could. Twenty-one days are twenty-one days."

"He has not eaten because of the sickness?"

"Well, true. His appetite is very poor. But aside from that, there is something else. Let me explain. Frate Pio does not eat because he prays without interruption. He continues to pray as if he did not need anything but prayer as nourishment of both spirit and body. Not to eat is against the seminary rules, you understand. We have other novices here and an example like the one Frate Pio gives could be damaging to their health. We have begged him to . . . well, we have begged him to stop praying and take some food. We love him. But he has refused to interrupt his fasting. We do not know what to do. We wonder how he keeps up enough strength to rise from his knees."

"Has the boy offended you then?" asked Orazio, more pained than ever. "Can he never return?"

"You misunderstand me," Father Agostino said. "Frate Pio offends no one. Only his own health. If he . . ." his voice broke, and he paused. "Well, if he *were* to recover," he said at last, "we would welcome him back, and with all our hearts."

For a moment the two men were silent together. Then the monk composed himself, drying his eyes. "I am sorry," he said. "I will call him now."

Father Agostino left the waiting room and returned with Frate Pio who stood in silence at his side. Frate Pio glanced at his father's face once, then lowered his eyes.

Orazio's astonishment and fear became crushing pain. His son was not even looking at him, let alone speaking to him. The Guardian Brother said, "Frate Pio, look up. You can freely speak to your father." Only then did Frate Pio embrace his father, clasping him long to his chest and crying, "I did not know you were back, I did not."

"But my son, you have reduced yourself like this?" sobbed Orazio at the sight of the sunken cheeks, eyes set deep in the rim of the sockets, a glow of blazing fever above the youthful beard.

"No food for twenty-one days!" Orazio exclaimed. "But you'll die. Hunger will kill you. How can it be, all those days without food?" He kissed Father Agostino's hand, whispering, "I take him home. He will be well again, I'll see to that. I do not know how but he must get well again. Maybe the air of our Pietrelcina. It is a matter of lungs, is it not? Then air counts."

But when Orazio arrived at the farmhouse, Frate Pio was not with him.

Maria Giuseppe, who expected her son to be very sick, and with him, was horrified when Orazio returned alone. But he quickly reassured her. On the way home, he explained, Piuccio had decided to stop off for a visit to his married sister Felicia.

"You mean," Maria Giuseppe cried, "the boy has gone visit-

ing?" Orazio shrugged. "Where does he get the strength?"
they asked one another.

"He must get to bed at once," said Maria Giuseppe.

Orazio, who had sent word ahead only that he was bringing
his son home, began to tell her the details of the bad news
Father Agostino had given him. Husband and wife were dis-
traught, and wept together. While they tried to comfort one
another, Frate Pio entered the house. He walked into the
kitchen, startling his parents in the midst of their laments.

"I am very hungry," he said jovially. "What are you cooking?"

Maria Giuseppe had not known what to prepare for the
invalid, and had begun a simple meal consisting only of turnips, with hot peppers for flavor and some leaves of radish, for
her own supper and Orazio's. When Piuccio saw the turnips,
he exclaimed, "Exactly what I wanted!" Then he sat down
at the table and ate the whole family's supper all by himself.

The family could not believe what they were seeing. His
face did not match Orazio's description or the words of Father
Agostino in the least. They looked at him in wonder. Orazio
sat perfectly still, his eyes wide at the sudden transformation.

When he finished eating, Frate Pio said, "I have already
made up for what I did not eat those twenty-one days."

The archpriest brought a doctor to the house. Dr. Ferrante
was an elderly man, and a man of generous sympathy. When
illness struck a home, Dr. Ferrante considered it his obligation
to visit every day if need be, until his patient recovered.

He found no sign of tuberculosis in Frate Pio. More sur-
prisingly, the patient's temperature was normal. The most

alarming aspect of Father Agostino's report had been his description of the extraordinary fevers the young student suffered. They would strike him every evening as the sun began to go down, and always, the thermometer would register temperatures well over a hundred. Yet in a few hours, the fever would subside, only to begin again next evening. Orazio and Maria Giuseppe were far too pleased by the doctor's opinion to wonder at the strangeness of the sudden change.

But the doctor had words of warning, too. Frate Pio was not to spend hours locked in his room, praying and studying, no matter how he wished to. He must get out of the house, walk in the country air, and exercise to improve his appetite.

But Frate Pio would not long remain idle and carefree. Since he was feeling well already, he saw no reason for staying away from the monastery. The cartman who had first driven him to Morcone offered to take him there again, and he gladly accepted. On the way, the cartman said to him, "They are calling me a liar in the Piazza because I said that when I saw you, you looked very sick, and now they saw for themselves and you don't look sick, you look well."

A few days before leaving for America, Orazio had a message from Father Agostino. "Your son's health is gaining rapidly," the Guardian Brother wrote, "and you should not worry now because what he eats is sufficient."

But Orazio was not convinced and asked that his son be allowed to spend some time in Pietrelcina where Maria Giuseppe could take care of him. When the Guardian Brother gently refused Orazio's request, the worried father repeated

it. Again Father Agostino declined, this time directing his
reply to the archpriest, to whom he explained that Frate Pio
would not be allowed to leave the monastery again without
the permission of the Provincial Father.

At this time, Frate Pio's health was good enough so that he
might safely continue his preparation for the priesthood. The
road ahead was a long one, requiring years of study. To date,
the boy had only his grammar school diploma. Secondary
education and courses equivalent to those given in universities
must be completed before Frate Pio's priestly ambition could
begin to be realized. The educational process would require
him to live and study in several different monastic institutions.

Orazio resigned himself to his son's continued absence from
home. But he remained worried. When he heard, shortly before he left again for America, that Piuccio had been trans-
ferred to another monastery, his concern was boundless. This
new home of his son's, at Saint Elia a Pianisi, was far more
remote, even, than Morcone had been. At least Morcone had
been near a good size town and had lain on a regional road. It
was not too far from Pietrelcina. But Saint Elia a Pianisi was
far away from Pietrelcina. It lay northeast of Campobasso,
between two secondary roads. Its position near the top of a
lofty mountain was utterly isolated.

Orazio was downcast at the news, but there was nothing he
could do. He left Pietrelcina for Naples and the ship to America with a heavy heart.

The good Don Salvatore had promised, when Orazio left,
to look after young Frate Pio, and make certain he needed
for nothing. Not long after the boy's transfer to Saint Elia a

Pianisi, the archpriest had disturbing news of his charge. The Guardian Brother at the new monastery wrote that Frate Pio was seriously ill. In the evening he would enter the study hall, and he would pass the rest of the night on his books. He had no regard whatever for his health. "He is very sick, with high fevers, and still does not abandon his studies," wrote the Brother. "We do not know what to do. It is a problem."

The archpriest well understood the consternation of the Superior at Saint Elia a Pianisi. In case of emergency the monks could not very well provide Frate Pio with speedy medical care. The letter ended, "His spirit, high and strong, seems to control the fever."

Then the thermometer cracked.

Don Salvatore was informed at once. As soon as the fever went down, Frate Pio would be leaving for another monastery even higher in the mountains, where the air was more favorable than at Saint Elia a Pianisi.

The new monastery was Venafro. It was far from Saint Elia a Pianisi, far from Morcone and Pietrelcina. Venafro overlooked Monte Cassino, and on clear days the monastery there could be seen in a distant outline.

It saddened Don Salvatore deeply that Piuccio was moved about without letup. At times, while he sat at the reading table in his bedroom, he would think of Piuccio and tears would blur his eyes. If only Frate Pio would not concentrate on the spirit to the complete exclusion of the body. "Rise and pray, lest you enter into temptation," Jesus said. Frate Pio of Pietrelcina accordingly rose and prayed almost without interruption. He endured periods of penance that seemed ab-

solute. Out of each one, he would emerge with a normal temperature, but his strength was gone, and his weight dangerously low. During the last penance he had not eaten for fifteen
days.

Pietrelcina knew what Frate Pio was doing. Villagers, when
they met the archpriest, would ask in a tone of disconsolate
and utterly compassionate mourning, "How is poor Fra Pio
now?"

One day, Don Salvatore had a startling answer to the ques-
tion. "The monks in Venafro are sending him home," he announced. He well understood their tone of mourning. It
served them to express their love.

When Frate Pio arrived at home again and visited the archpriest in the church of Saint Mary of the Angels, Don Salvatore could not decide for a long moment if the boy looked ill
or well. Except for his pallor and thinness, there was no other
indication. His face, perfectly serene, reflected his happy
spirit.

Frate Pio was radiant as he informed the archpriest that he
had earned his secondary school and junior college diplomas
at Morcone, Saint Elia a Pianisi, and Venafro. Now he was
free to stay home all summer. In the fall, he would go to the
seminary of Saint Mark in Catola for the course of philosophy.
This was the next step. His voice sounded as his eyes looked,
happy. He talked with joy about the next effort, and the
next. Before he would be a priest, he must return for a second
period to Saint Elia a Pianisi. Then there would be four years
of theology in two seminaries, Serracapriola and Montefusco,
in the crowded province of Avellino.

"But, Piuccio, your health?" asked the archpriest.

"Well, if I stopped to think of it that would only slow down my studies," he answered. He spoke lovingly of the monasteries he had lived in. His affection was not simply for the isolation, or for the lofty structures around which clouds hovered like crowns. What he loved so was the life inside those walls, the prayer and meditation, the brotherhood in Christ.

Maria Giuseppe asked the archpriest whether Piuccio would agree to be a priest in Pietrelcina, once he was ordained. In turn, in his shy, tentative way, Don Salvatore asked Frate Pio. "It would be only wise, considering how often you have felt much better here," he said.

The answer was no. Frate Pio did not wish to leave the Order of the Franciscan Brothers.

"Anyway, there is time," said Don Salvatore.

"It will be the same answer later," said Frate Pio. He would not abandon a road on which he was so deeply involved, would not choose again once he had chosen. "There are today ten thousand monks. I am one of them, and one of them I will be up to the last."

For Maria Giuseppe, summer went all too quickly. She cared for her boy as best she could, but nothing she could say or do would keep him from praying through the long nights. Yet, when autumn came, he was well. The people of Pietrelcina saw, and began to speak among themselves of a monk who cured himself of tuberculosis by praying.

When the days began to grow short, Frate Pio bade his

mother and sisters and brother, and the kindly archpriest, a fond good-by, and left for Saint Mark in Catola in the province of Foggia, more prosperous by far than the environs of Pietrelcina. Small villages were few, and large farm towns rose on seemingly endless acres of rich wheat land. The cattle were fat and plenty, and the land was a dark, fertile brown— the same color as his robe.

It was at Saint Mark in Catola, in the province of Foggia, that Frate Pio began to seek complete purity of thought. In the enacting of this resolution, he confronted painful obstacles. It was the first time he struggled with temptation.

Work and prayer were his remedy. He did well with his philosophy studies, and completed the course at Saint Mark in Catola. Then he returned to Saint Elia a Pianisi, for his second sojourn there. It was there that temptations took solid shapes in his eyes.

One night, in his cell adjoining the cell of Brother Anastasio, he saw a monstrous dog on Brother Anastasio's cot. Before his eyes, the dog leaped from the cot to the window sill, then out into the summer night. It's lean body was illuminated like a firefly. The sight terrified Frate Pio, and he collapsed on his cot. He spoke to no one of his experience.

In 1907, after his course at Saint Elia a Pianisi, Frate Pio came home to Pietrelcina for a short visit. He was as delighted to see his family and friends as they were to see him. But it was not long before they noticed that something was wrong.

Piuccio would spend the early part of the evening with Don Salvatore, but at nine-thirty every night, he would retire to his room. Night after night, at that hour, family, friends, and neighbors heard cries and screams, and the sounds of solid bodies hitting the floor.

On the first such occasion, Frate Pio's family rushed to his room and threw open the door. There they saw books and ink well thrown about, chairs upside down on the floor, bed blankets scattered around the room, the walls stained with ink. Frate Pio, standing in the midst of the confusion, was silent. He motioned to his family to leave the room, and closed the door and bolted it when they were barely at the other side of the threshold.

When Orazio arrived for a short visit, his wife and son and daughters and neighbors told him of the frightful screams that they heard every evening at nine-thirty.

"You will hear, unless it does not happen tonight," said Maria Giuseppe.

"But what is it?" asked Orazio. "It is said that one finds strange things in America, but then I come home and find really strange things."

Frate Pio was always alone in his room when the disturbances took place. He had made it clear that he did not want his family to be with him, and they respected his wishes. But one evening, while Frate Pio was in church with Don Salvatore, Orazio entered the room. It was a little before nine-thirty. At the sight of the ink-stained walls Orazio took fright and ran out of the room to the front door. He stopped just inside the threshold, forcing himself to stay in the house so his neighbors would not see how terrified he was. There he stood, waiting for Piuccio to come home from church. When

Frate Pio appeared, a booming voice inside the house said: "Here comes the Holy."

Orazio trembled, but stayed where he was. When Frate Pio entered, the same booming voice pronounced the same words, and Frate Pio answered quietly, "Yes, I am back home."

Spent with fright, Orazio cried, "What is it, what happens?"

The rest of the family, following Frate Pio into the house, joined their pleas with Orazio's. "Tell your father what happens."

But Frate Pio, silent, entered his room and bolted the door.

Orazio said, "Oh, Lord. Truly this poor Christian stands between here and the beyond."

Then Frate Pio found two words that brought complete silence, even in the midst of the most incredible noise and violence. Every evening, when the quiet was shattered, Frate Pio said the two words: "*Viva Gesù!*" At the word Jesus, silence returned.

Orazio confided to Don Salvatore the trials Frate Pio was enduring, and the archpriest was both baffled and afraid for his protégé. He wondered whether such extraordinary events had occurred at the monasteries Piuccio had lived in, too. He wrote to Father Agostino at Morcone, asking the Guardian Brother to write and tell him if he knew of anything remarkable about Frate Pio, outside of the boy's illnesses. But there was no answer.

Father Agostino's failure to respond made Don Salvatore even more curious. He knew that Piuccio had himself written to his first Guardian Brother and he asked the boy to bring him Father Agostino's answer when it arrived. Frate Pio cheerfully agreed, and a few days later, appeared at the church of Saint Mary of the Angels with his first letter from Father Agostino. Frate Pio had not opened the envelope, but presented it to Don Salvatore exactly as it had arrived. Don Salvatore broke the seal and drew from the envelope a single folded sheet of paper. It was perfectly blank.

"Look what Father Agostino has done. He has forgotten to write the letter and only folded this sheet in the envelope, with nothing written on it," said Don Salvatore.

Frate Pio took the blank sheet and looked at it. "No, he did not forget to write. He wrote on this sheet, but those *signori* have played me one more of their tricks. The words are here, but they have been crossed out by the devil. I can tell you what is written on this sheet." And he told Don Salvatore what Father Agostino had written.

"Piuccio, listen to me. The devil can do just what you said, cross out a letter. That is, he can make the words disappear, or fade them to the point that they are no longer visible to the eyes. But too, you could have opened the envelope and taken Father Agostino's letter, and placed this blank sheet here. Mind you, I believe you would not do such a thing, but still, for my complete peace of mind, I must find out.

"I will write a letter to Father Agostino and I will ask him to repeat this letter, and I will send this blank sheet along, so that Father Agostino can tell me if this is the sheet on which he wrote. In this manner there will be no doubt."

"Do as you say," said Frate Pio. "You have every right to complete peace of mind."

Don Salvatore wrote and asked. Soon the answer came. The sheet did belong to Father Agostino, and it was the same sheet on which he had written the letter which Frate Pio had quoted.

Don Salvatore called Frate Pio and said, "You are right. Furthermore, something else has happened. I have received another letter from Father Agostino. The sheet had nothing on it but a splash of ink, in the shape of a funnel. Nothing else. I called my niece and I said to her, 'Do you also see a splash of ink here and nothing else? No words? Is there anything here but a large splash of ink in the shape of a funnel?' "

His niece had looked at the letter carefully, and she had agreed with him.

The good archpriest had then stepped into the church and had sprinkled holy water on the sheet. The handwriting of Father Agostino had appeared. For a long moment Don Salvatore had stood with the letter in his hands, not daring to think. He had spoken to Frate Pio about his peace of mind, and now proof had been doubly furnished. Now he had his peace of mind because he believed. Well, it was not the first time in history that devils tried to deviate a man of God. This, after all, was nothing new. It was happening to Frate Pio of Pietrelcina precisely because he had never indicated any weakness in his devotion to God.

When Maria Giuseppe visited the archpriest and expressed wonder at Pio's experiences, Don Salvatore repeated to her what Frate Pio himself had once said. "The devil is like a mad dog tied to a chain. Beyond the limit of the chain the dog cannot go, so you should stay far from where the chain reaches or you will be hurt. The devil has only one door to enter, and in your soul that door is called will. There are no hidden doors."

Day after day Frate Pio knelt in the little straw hut alongside the farmhouse. He did not touch food, but only wet his lips with drinking water from a primitive earthenware container that stood beside him on the naked floor of the hut. Nearby, his mother worked in the fields. Often, while she worked, she was interrupted by people who spoke to her of Pietrelcina's recuperative powers, the benefits of its air and drinking water. They urged her to bear in mind the quality of Pietrelcina's vegetables. Finally, they pointed out that Frate Pio became ill when he was away from home and that, therefore, she should not allow him to go to Montefusco.

"My son does what his heart dictates," she would answer.

Soon it would be sundown again, and the battle resumed in Frate Pio's room at nine-thirty. To spare his family, he began to sleep in the hut, on the dirt floor. There he struggled now.

Pietrelcina spoke of the noises "that come from the home of the monk." Soon, nearby towns were talking about *lu monaco* of Pietrelcina.

The sick man "who is well again," the monk who did not mind suffering "because we all suffer," the "monk who suffers more than we do and is well and looks strong," was the center of attention.

He did not want any attention. He called himself "this

worthless servant of Jesus" and did not wish to attract people
to him. What he wanted was to pray on his knees, to study,
to become a priest.

He believed that prayer "should be insistent as the fact of
insisting would denote faith," so he prayed long. He believed
that prayer "is the best arm we have, and it is a key which
opens the heart of the Lord," so he prayed often.

His will, however, was perfectly nonexistent to the people
of Pietrelcina whose needs, both material and spiritual, were
like a forest fire, all-devouring. Such needs could blot out completely the God-loving and humble wish not to receive any
attention.

The people of Pietrelcina loved Frate Pio, and they were
proud of him. They wanted him to stay in their town, to pray
his prayers among them.

"We have nothing," they would say to him. "All we have
is you." And Frate Pio wept.

Just the same he planned to leave for Montefusco, in Avellino Province. The next time he would return to Pietrelcina,
he would come as Padre Pio.

Chapter 4

O<small>N</small> A<small>UGUST</small> 10, 1910, in the cathedral of Benevento, Frate Pio of Pietrelcina was ordained priest. The Bishop of Benevento put his hands on his head, invoking the Holy Ghost, and Frate Pio became Padre Pio. As he said his first Mass in the cathedral his eyes filled with tears. Maria Giuseppe, his brother, Michele, his sisters, Felicia and Grazia, and Don Salvatore, the archpriest of Pietrelcina, watched the candlelight shine in his blurred eyes.

Seven years before, he had donned his brown robe and his white sash, and started on the road that had led him to this morning. He was twenty-three years old. He had triumphed over illness until it had ceased to worry him or his superiors in the monastic order. For the rest of his life, the privilege of saying Mass would be his.

People of Benevento and nearby towns, people who knew of his powerful dedication to prayer and meditation, flocked to hear his first Mass. Only Orazio, far away in America, was missing. The people saw that Padre Pio was in good health, and the archpriest made a special mental note of that. Only recently the superiors at the Montefusco seminary had notified him that the last two years of hard study had left Frate Pio too weak to endure the strain of final examinations. But at the very last minute, he had stepped to the heavy cart which was to carry the tense students to the examinations and had pleaded with his superior, "Let me ride, I am too weak to walk." The cart was already filled. But in a flash of compassion and generosity another student jumped off. After the tests, Frate Pio walked back to the monastery. The road seemed twice its length because of his weakness. He returned late, and found that the other students already knew that he had passed all his exams brilliantly.

After the celebration of the Mass, his mother stopped calling him Piuccio and began addressing him as Padre Pio, making her voice as formal as the words. In her formality there was harsh, country-folk pride. Their way parted at the end of the Mass. The group of relatives returned to Pietrelcina, Padre Pio to Montefusco, in the thickly populated province of Avellino.

He was a priest. If he so wished, he could stay in Pietrelcina and help Don Salvatore in Saint Mary of the Angels, instead of journeying from place to place, as monks did, in continual peregrination. He could stay in his native hamlet, where the air was so beneficial for his lungs. But Padre Pio had other plans. In the oppressive heat of August, when the plains shimmered in the sunlight, he went back to Montefusco.

Padre Pio would often say, "Our body is like a donkey. We beat him, but with some consideration. Otherwise he throws himself on the ground and will not carry us anymore." Yet he undertook such penances, fasting and praying day and night before the Cross, that again his temperature could not be registered with an ordinary thermometer. Nobody had ever heard of such fevers. In consternation, the Montefusco monks thought of no other solution than the usual: back again to Pietrelcina.

The people of his town turned out in the Square to greet him as though they were attending a funeral. When the cart came, the driver had to help him down.

This time the monks' attempt to cure Padre Pio by sending him home was a failure. Only God could bring relief to the suffering people of the world. To Padre Pio, it made no difference whether he was in Montefusco or Pietrelcina. He fasted and prayed, as always, silently enduring his fevers as he knelt, begging the Lord's mercy on his people. He did not leave the straw hut except to say Mass. In the newspapers and on the lips of people, there was talk of war. In seclusion in his hut, Padre Pio sent his prayers to heaven, pleading for peace.

One day a number of women of Pietrelcina appeared in the rectory of Saint Mary of the Angels and began to complain to Don Salvatore. They spoke haltingly and in whispers. It seemed that they did not really wish to speak at all.

"We are country people," one of them announced at last.

"We are called to the weeding, now that harvest is over," said another.

"We have landowners who are pressed for our work."

Impatiently, Don Salvatore said, "Yes, yes, I know you must work. What have I to do with that? What is the matter?"

"*Lu monaco.*"

"Padre Pio. Well, go on."

"His Mass lasts too long. *Lu monaco* has such a long Mass that . . ."

"A good Mass goes fast, and surely he says a good Mass," said Don Salvatore.

The women agreed at once, and fell into constrained silence. Then one gathered up her courage and explained that they did not mean to hinder the love of Jesus in the heart of the young priest, but work called them. Animals, tools, earth, ashes required their attention. They could not in this season, although they might in full winter, wait for the end of the Padre Pio Mass.

They concluded, speaking in unison, "His Mass never ends. We do not know what to do, wait for the end and be late for work or . . ."

At certain points in the Mass the dialogue between the celebrant and God was transformed into timeless love. The face of the celebrant, transformed in pain and sorrow, was streaked with tears in the special privilege of the priest who could relive the Passion of Jesus Christ. Padre Pio's rapture was evident when he kissed the altar the first time, again at the words "Cleanse my heart," and most of all at the offer of the Bread and Wine, and from the Consecration to the Communion.

The Mass lasted three hours.

People stood wide-eyed. They wept.

In utter simplicity, above all a humble servant of God, Padre Pio had no idea how much time was going by. At the end of the Mass, he would kneel behind the altar and pray silently, never aware of whether he was watched or was alone.

Often the sacristan would leave and return later, to find him still in the same place. Once he found that Padre Pio had fainted. He did not dare touch him, but ran to call Don Salvatore, and the archpriest helped Padre Pio to his feet and into the sacristy.

But even though they understood that Padre Pio did not know the difference between minutes and hours, the country people could not afford to spend three hours at Mass.

The archpriest pondered upon the situation, but no ready solution occurred to him. The son of Orazio Forgione knew well the demanding schedule of farming. If only he knew what time it was!

Then the archpriest had an idea. Alone in the church one day, he said aloud, "My dear Padre Pio, you are a monk and you have the vow of obedience. I hold here the place of your superior. Therefore I shall command you to make the Mass short. I shall command you mentally, and let us hope you get the message." He was thinking that the angels, as messengers of Our Lord, would help him.

What happened at the next Mass astonished him. The moment Padre Pio touched the altar and was about to begin his unawareness of time, he was called back to reality.

The people of Pietrelcina were sure Don Salvatore had asked Padre Pio to keep the Mass short, and it upset the good Father not to be able to tell them what had really happened.

In the kingdom of the downtrodden, in the little town of Pietrelcina, Padre Pio prayed to the Lord for relief and blessing.

He had been their *Frate* and now was their priest. His language was their own Neapolitan dialect. Always they had lived in pain and fear, with sickness and starvation constant companions, the landowners' wrath their constant dread. Now they had a new cause for trembling. War was close. Nobody knew just when it would break out, but come it would. Young and old alike would be asked to shed their clothes and forsake their homes for a pair of puttees and a trench. In the far North, on Italian territory, Austria still held sway. Peace was a word. The fact was not peace. Every day that there was no war was merely a day that the war was postponed. Then Archduke Ferdinand was murdered in Sarajevo, and the powder keg exploded. Italy was in a war.

The people of the South were simple folk, who knew little of archdukes and empires. The rules that guided their lives and sustained their spirits were not laws of a land, but ancient, wholesome customs. They lived in the houses of their grandfathers, surely never in a rented house. They put to their lips no other liquid than the wine they made with their own hands and the water of their own springs. They would don garments only to protect themselves from the bad weather or the killing heat, and never for show or vanity. They had and wanted no other heat in their houses than that of their own logs, chopped with their own hands. They made full use of daylight for the purpose of labor, and neither could nor would labor after sundown. They made all payments in kind and never dreamed of using money, because they were wary of money like any other manufactured goods. They kept out of the way of strangers,

and turned their backs to politics, which they saw as the work
of the devil.

These were the men of the South, called to put on puttees
and live in trenches.

They turned to their church and their saints. In Pietrelcina,
they turned to their own Neapolitan priest. People ran up to
him in the church of Saint Mary of the Angels, begging him
to make one more appeal to the Lord. But Padre Pio was not
to remain long at Pietrelcina. One day, the postman came to
Saint Mary of the Angels with a postal card for Padre Pio.
King Victor Emmanuel III was calling Francesco Forgione to
the army district of Naples for a medical examination.

Army doctors found Padre Pio sound from head to foot.
The Naples district ordered him to take off his robe and don
the gray-green uniform of an Italian soldier. Nobody paused
a moment to indicate the line in which he was to stand. For
all appearances, he was a soldier like another. No one knew
that there was this difference: the others prayed for themselves, Padre Pio prayed for them. Padre Pio was not sent to
the trenches, nor was he asked to kill fellow human beings. He
was stationed in a hospital, the Trinita dei Monti, in Naples.

The city whose name he had so often heard, since the earliest
days of his childhood, was tragically poor. The streets were
teeming with people, all of whom seemed to live in the most
abject poverty. Here there were none of the blessings of land
and space that the peasants of Pietrelcina enjoyed. The citizens
were pressed into homes too small to contain them, and their

wan discouragement showed that they suffered oppression of spirit as well as of body.

Padre Pio saw these people, and he wept. When he returned to his post at the Trinita dei Monti hospital, he went to bed with a high fever, as though the misery of Naples had brought it on.

His temperature rose so high that the doctors in gray-green were able to measure it only with a bath thermometer. This soldier with the perfectly serene eyes, they declared, had fevers that were incredible. Yet Padre Pio astonished nurses and doctors by rising from his bed every day to discharge his duties as hospital orderly.

In the long bare corridors, alive with moaning, he pronounced a prayer for each step he took. While others slept, their wounds medicated, Padre Pio prayed to the Lord for humanity.

The soul, that was the catalyst. He prayed for the souls of his patients, and then comforted them with words of home. He himself turned to eager remembrances of the naked altars of all the monasteries, with their little countryside churches, he had lived in.

Seated on his cot, he wrote long letters to Pietrelcina, to people who were sick and beyond medical hope. His letters, which started with the words "Peace, Pity, and Grace," delivered an immediate courage. In one of the letters, he said, "I was assured that your health was somewhat improved. The news filled me with joy, but a sadness gripped me because of your prolonged silence, which let me believe that once again I was tricked by the demon." In another letter he spoke of the

Epistle to the Philippians, "To understand the Apostle it is necessary to consider his state at the time of the Epistle. He was in Rome, a prisoner, because he had preached the Gospel while Nero was Emperor. So, he was suspended between life and death, although it could be that he would gain his freedom again, as it happened. He first of all declared to the faithful that he was ready for anything for the love of God, and, as he had faith, he considered his chains also as advantageous for his eternal life." How personal this message was to become!

The military knew that Francesco Forgione had been sound when he reported for service, as their own records showed. Now he was tubercular. How could Francesco Forgione live with such temperatures?

He was given a sick leave.

A few weeks later, the authorities at the hospital of the Trinita dei Monti dispatched a postal card to Francesco Forgione of Pietrelcina, informing him that his leave was over and he was to return to the service. But Francesco Forgione was not in Pietrelcina. The postman of Pietrelcina respectfully returned the postal card to the authorities with that notation. Then the king's police began looking for Francesco Forgione.

The marshal of Pietrelcina went to Maria Giuseppe and to Felicia, the married sister.

"He is not here," Felicia said. "His superiors sent him to San Giovanni Rotondo, near Foggia, where they said the air is good for him. He is there now, just returned from Rome where he has accompanied my sister Grazia to the convent of the Brigidine Sisters, for she will become a nun."

"San Giovanni Rotondo?"

"Yes, near Foggia."

"So then all I need do is send his papers to Foggia, because if San Giovanni Rotondo is near Foggia, the marshal in Foggia will send the papers to the marshal in San Giovanni Rotondo."

"I guess so. But I can assure you he is in San Giovanni Rotondo now."

The marshal sent the papers to the Foggia *carabinieri*. A superficial inquiry about soldier Forgione resulted in a report to Naples that there was no soldier by that name in San Giovanni Rotondo.

The Naples district issued the order of arrest for desertion, punishment death. It was up to the king's police to find the deserter, carry out the order of arrest, and ship him to the prison of Gaeta. Mandate followed mandate from the military district, and the police in Foggia pressed the police in San Giovanni Rotondo. People in San Giovanni Rotondo shrugged their shoulders and shook their heads. They did not know this man named Francesco Forgione.

"Surely you know yourself, marshal, that in this town we do not have a family named Forgione."

"Of course I know we do not."

"Stop looking then."

"How can I? Naples and Foggia are sure he lives here."

"Well, keep on looking until they forget the whole thing."

"Never. He is a deserter."

"He is nobody since he does not exist."

"For us he does not but for them he does. And in addition for them he exists right here in San Giovanni Rotondo. So that it is my duty...."

"Impossible. It is incredible that they order you to send to Gaeta nobody."

The police, rifle mouths down from the shoulder, tramped the fields, from farmhouse to farmhouse. Then they sent the papers back to Foggia and the marshal in Foggia sent them back to Pietrelcina.

The marshal asked Maria Giuseppe, "But where is he?"

"In San Giovanni Rotondo."

"Are you sure?"

"I am sure. Why do you ask, is there anything wrong?"

"Wrong?"

The papers were sent to Foggia and this time, handcuffs ready, the police were put on a lonely path on a piece of land called Patariello, nothing more than a twist on the trail. They were still searching for Francesco Forgione, a deserter to be brought to the prison of Gaeta. Then the path started to grip the ribs of the mountain. In the *bora*, the fierce wind from the Adriatic Sea, there rose at the end of the path the church of Saint Mary of the Graces behind a cobbled clearing.

"Well, no use. Just the monks live here. We know them one by one and it is not respectful to disturb them with our problems. Let us go back to San Giovanni Rotondo," said the marshal to his troopers.

But just then the door of the monastery opened, a friar appeared wrapped in the wind. "*Sia lodato Gesù Cristo,*" he said.

It was Father Gaudenzio.

"No wind for Christians," said the marshal. "But duty is duty. We are looking for a man named Francesco Forgione."

"Who?"

"His name is Francesco Forgione, son of Orazio, and he lives here in Patariello, here somewhere, but there are no houses here. He is a man from Pietrelcina."

"Pietrelcina? Yes, he is Padre Pio."

"Padre Pio? Isn't Padre Pio Padre Pio?"

"Yes, but before his name was Forgione."

"So then it is the same person? We have been hearing the Mass and making Communion with Padre Pio and all the time these papers were in my pocket."

"What papers?"

"Nothing. It is nothing. Please tell Padre Pio to go to Naples. I have here documents not delivered to him because the name is Francesco Forgione on the papers. The first card says that his sick leave is over, was over a long time ago. It was not delivered and so he does not know that he should have been back. Here is the card. Please give it to him."

"Wait," said Father Gaudenzio. "I call Padre Pio."

"Do not disturb him. It is not at all his fault."

"*Sia lodato Gesù Cristo*," said Father Gaudenzio, and closed the door.

In the hospital in Naples, the colonel who had sent out the search, the captain, and the noncommissioned officers in the orderly room looked up when Forgione entered. No one of them said a word. Before their amazed eyes stood a young man of skin and bones, tuberculosis obvious on his face. Then the Colonel spoke: "My son, I'll put in for your discharge. Since our records show that you were not sick when you were drafted, I'll petition a pension of war for you. Expect to go back home shortly."

Padre Pio said, "Why should I have a war pension?" What had he done that should be compensated with ribbons, medals, a war pension? "I was sick before," he said.

"You were well when we drafted you." The colonel dismissed him.

Padre Pio returned to his robe, sash, and sandals. He returned to the hut next door to his quiet house in Pietrelcina, vacant now except for his mother, because Grazia was a nun in Rome, Felicia and Michele were married, and Orazio was in America. Here, in the faint echoes of the days when the whole family used to gather around the supper table in the humble kitchen, he settled down to wait until his superiors sent for him. Perhaps they would give him permission to return to San Giovanni Rotondo. Then again, perhaps they would send him here and there, to say a Mass one day in one town and the next day in another, to gladden the hearts of the faithful in isolated spots.

He re-entered the hut next door to kneel in the silence of the remote hills, sadly populated now with the sorrows of a nation at war. Trains bearing wounded arrived from the North, telegraph offices delivered black-bordered wires.

And he helped Don Salvatore, his father and brother and mentor and companion, in Saint Mary of the Angels. A Mass for the dead, a Mass for a boy of Pietrelcina who only yesterday, with honor and dignity, had waved his military cap, saying good-by to his children, his wife and mother and father,

a Mass for the Unknown Soldier. Then Padre Pio would
make his way, along the solitary paths, back up the hill from
Saint Mary of the Angels to pray all evening long. Next
morning, long before sunrise, he would be on his knees again
asking the Almighty to lighten the human burden.

In the grips of their tragedy the people sought out the
young *Padre* with the serene eyes and the calm, strong face.
Mothers and brides who could not stop weeping came to him
for comfort. His own deep courage helped them.

Then his superiors ordered him to spend a few weeks in
Saint Mark in Catola, and he went. His health was improved,
and he was able to undertake monastic peregrinations from one
nearby church to another. And from time to time he returned
to Pietrelcina. Once again the archpriest proposed that Padre
Pio should establish himself in Saint Mary of the Angels. Said
Don Salvatore, "As your mother has suggested to me, I have
asked the Capuchins to release you from the hard rules of the
order, and here is a paper which represents the permission.
You stay here. It will be a life better suited to your health. I
am old, and you can help me in the parish."

"*Zi Tore*, I was five years old when I swore loyalty to San
Francesco. I cannot take my word back. I have planned to
ask for permanent residence in San Giovanni Rotondo. It will
take a little while for the answer, and I shall wait here for it."

It was the last time Don Salvatore was to ask him to stay.
On September 17, 1915, conclusive evidence of Pio's mission
was given, evidence that Don Salvatore took as a message to
him that he should not try to hold Pio at Pietrelcina any
longer. That day was like any other, until his mother called

him for the midday meal. He did not answer, and she called again, and again, her voice echoing from the nearby mountain. Then suddenly, Padre Pio ran from the hut, waving his hands. He had been kneeling in prayer when he felt a fierce burning in his hands. He had looked for a bucket of water to dip his hands in, but found nothing. Then, still waving, he had rushed out of the hut. Now he was crossing the field to the house.

"Padre Pio," said his mother, "what are you doing, playing the guitar?" But when she saw the expression of pain on his face her voice changed, and she cried, "Padre Pio, what is the matter with your hands?"

He stopped, and lowered his eyes to his hands. Then slowly he turned around and started back to the hut.

Maria Giuseppe ran after him. When she entered the hut she found him already kneeling, hands joined, face uplifted. His face was contorted in agony. Maria Giuseppe ran out, down the path. She could still see the expression of pain on her son's face when she reached Saint Mary of the Angels. When she found the archpriest, she cried, "Something is happening to Padre Pio. He is in pain. I called him to eat and he came out of the hut waving his hands."

Don Salvatore was having his midday meal. "Fevers again?" He rose from the table and began looking for his hat.

"I do not know what it is this time, but it is something different. Oh, the way his face looks! Please hurry."

"I come."

Side by side they hurried through the fields to the path leading from the farmhouse to the hut. Maria Giuseppe pressed her kerchief to her mouth in fear, the archpriest's lips moved rapidly in prayer. Then they entered the hut.

Padre Pio's face was wet with tears. But his face showed less pain, as though the burning sensation had tried to overcome his spirit, but had failed. He dried his eyes. He looked up at his mother, then at the archpriest. "The pain is all gone," he said. "It is nothing. Do not worry."

"But what was it?" asked Don Salvatore.

"My hands were burning, right here in the palms."

"Burning?" The archpriest, without waiting for an answer, turned to the opening of the hut and stepped outside. There he whispered to Maria Giuseppe, "Let the Lord do what He wishes."

In the kitchen, Padre Pio sat at the table, but could not hold his fork. He put it down and sat motionless, in silence.

The archpriest soon called Maria Giuseppe to the rectory and said, "Be calm. If he still wishes to go back to San Giovanni Rotondo, let him go."

"Tell me what the burning is."

Don Salvatore spoke quietly. "He has received the invisible stigmata, the secret of the Lord. I for one wish to keep the secret a secret, Maria Giuseppe. That is to say, a letter from me to his superiors, to San Giovanni Rotondo where he wishes to establish himself permanently, would strengthen the point that Piuccio is on the right path. But I will not write the letter because a secret is a secret. If the Lord wanted anyone else to know, He would have given him the invisible stigmata there in San Giovanni Rotondo, and not here in this hut. Yes, he takes this blessing to San Giovanni Rotondo, but it is clear to me that the Lord does not want San Giovanni Rotondo to know."

"But what are these stigmata?"

"A message from Jesus Christ to Padre Pio, that he has been chosen to suffer like Jesus on the Cross, so that his suffering is offered to humanity. That is to say, one man suffers for others, who are spared suffering. One man carries the burden."

She blinked. Then she wept.

In a few days Padre Pio went to Saint Mark in Catola and he stayed in that monastery until March 5, 1918. It was there that he received word from the superiors of the order that his request for permanent residence in San Giovanni Rotondo had been granted.

Chapter 5

Frst settlers in San Giovanni Rotondo had chosen the mountain in the hope that invading armies, discouraged by its height, would leave them alone. Later generations, often conquered in the centuries, did not abandon the town because they believed that mountain life made people strong, good air kept them healthy, seclusion brought meditation and enlarged wisdom.

When Padre Pio came to the town, a few houses grouped around a small, slanted, and cobblestoned piazza, it was mourning casualties. Strong soldiers who had breathed good air, had meditated in seclusion and enlarged their wisdom, had died and now were mourned.

Despite the war, the people of San Giovanni Rotondo still supported values which had endured a thousand years, and which, they hoped, would endure with no end at all.

The monastery, further up the mountain, stood alone. Nobody but the monks lived that far up.

There were six friars in Saint Mary of the Graces at that time, Brother Agostino, the Guardian Father; Brother Ferdinando, the oldest; and Brother Gaudenzio, Brother Nicola, Brother Carmelo, Brother Arcangelo. Whether they were young, middle-aged, or old, whether their faces were accented by black beards or white, people who visited the monastery were impressed by the sharp difference between their alert, bright faces and the faces of ordinary men. Their faces revealed quick minds, kind hearts, vigorous spirits. When new friars came to San Giovanni Rotondo, the same comment could be made of them too. It was as if only minds especially endowed would decide to embark on the monastic life.

If to others the rule of the convent founded as it was on spiritual tests bearing physical strain, seemed hard, it did not seem so to the Brothers of San Giovanni Rotondo. Their way of life was well suited to the stuff they were made of.

The Brothers offered the outside world all the consolations of the faith: Mass, Holy Communion, baptism, confession, and marriage services. Among themselves, they lived in true communion, one in their devotion. Yet each existed as a monk above all. Alone and in silence, each attended to the destiny of his soul. Their performance of pastoral and monastic duties had an ease gained from long practice. To them the rule did not even seem strict.

It was not by mere chance that the door of Saint Mary of the Graces was always left open. Two centuries ago, in the dead of winter, when only wolves crept to the door of the church, San Giovanni Rotondo had been engulfed in a blizzard. The snow fell for so long and rose to such a depth that the monks could not leave the monastery, nor could the people from the town reach them. From the windows of their cells, the friars could see endless miles of unbroken snow.

Their isolation went on interminably, so long that finally all
the supplies in the monastery kitchen were used up. The monks
could envision no solution to their plight, but in accordance
with the rule, they gathered just the same in the refectory.
Just as they sat down before their empty plates and bowed
their heads, the front bell rang and the wolves howled. The
monks peered out and beheld a man pulling a donkey, and the
donkey was laden with baskets. The man unloaded with tremendous haste and at once hurried out of sight down the
trail. Gathered around the baskets the monks thanked God.
For the rest of the winter they would have food.

In 1918 the monastery and Saint Mary of the Graces were
as of old, not at all changed since the day the man dumped
the baskets and hurried down the trail. Only the mountain
had changed. Then there had been trees, but decade after
decade, trees were chopped down for wood coal by the people
of San Giovanni Rotondo. So now, in 1918, not a single tree
shaded the mountain.

Inside the church, niches contained wooden scultpures of
Franciscan saints draped in red and yellow and violet, loud
colors selected by shepherds and cowherds. The statues and
their drapery were greatly admired by the people of San
Giovanni Rotondo who would spend hours gazing at the
man-sized saints in their golden glowing garments.

Padre Pio settled permanently in cell number five. Silently,
he endured the burning pain in his hands, the invisible stigmata
which only the archpriest of Pietrelcina and Maria Giuseppe

knew of. Periodically Padre Pio went into penances and fasting of fifteen and twenty days.

The six compassionate monks watched him in growing
amazement. Gently they tried to lessen his hardships and the
hard rules of the order. But at all times he firmly shook his
head, declining favors. Even when his fevers seemed to be
devouring him, he refused any exception to the rules. His
response when even slight attention was paid him because of
his obvious poor health was short and austere. It was nobody's
business but his own what kind of Cross Jesus had put on him.

His meals consisted of boiled greens. The monks were
astounded at his refusal to eat their simple but substantial fare.
Around San Giovanni Rotondo, the greens Padre Pio ate were
to be found growing wild and therefore cost nothing. People
of San Giovanni Rotondo soon heard about the new friar's
extreme piety, his compassionate way with the sick and suffering, and his long fasts. One day in that spring of 1918, as
he was sitting in the quiet garden with one of his visitors, he
expressed the wish for a plate of spaghetti. The man rose immediately from the garden wall and said in great haste, "I
return." He ran all the way to San Giovanni Rotondo, arriving
breathless and exhausted, to tell his wife to cook for Padre Pio.
He was soon back with a basket.

In cell number five he prepared the table, table-spread, and
napkin and fork and spoon, and then he produced the efforts
of his wife—a plate of spaghetti with tomato sauce. For himself he dished out his own meal, spaghetti with garlic and oil.
They sat around the small table and Padre Pio lifted his hand

for the sign of the Cross. He held his hand over the food for a moment, then lowered it to his lap.

"It would be better if you brought all this nice food to the poor. It is dinner time now and you will find plenty of tables in town with a piece of bread and nothing else. Put all this back in the basket and go to them."

The man sat downhearted. Then he muttered, "If you wish," and he packed his basket again. On the way out he met Brother Carmelo. "He did not eat."

"What happened?"

"At the last minute he changed his mind for the poor."

"So it is," sighed the Brother.

Brother Carmelo talked to Padre Pio about his diet. He and the other monks felt miserable at the thought of Padre Pio's meals when they sat down in the refectory. Not that they ate much, but they ate.

Padre Pio considered their feelings and agreed to improve his diet, adding lemon juice to go with the boiled vegetables, and a glass of beer. The beer, a sort of luxury, made the other monks feel happier. But Padre Pio was free to decide what to eat out of the available supply, and soon he eliminated the beer and returned to greens pure and simple.

In the evening, in his cell, he wrote long letters of comfort to those who needed his help but could not reach the monastery. The letters were five and six pages long. "Do not fear. Have faith. Do not give in to fears you yourself create. For the sons of the Lord there is no distance ... Jesus says it in His Gospel: only those who obey the will of His Father are

His Brothers. In the spiritual life you must sail on, never take a step back, otherwise it will be as it is with the sailboat which, if stopped, will go at random according to the wind."

With the spring, people came to answer in person. Out of his deep understanding of suffering and sorrow, he spoke to them at length of hope and courage and God's mercy.

A few men began to come every day at the same hour, and they sat quietly in the garden with Padre Pio. After half an hour they would rise and depart. To the people of San Giovanni Rotondo, they would say, "We feel happy when we are in the company of Padre Pio."

But to people who came to Saint Mary of the Graces only out of curiosity, Padre Pio would use few words, short, final words, such as to say, "Go away."

Some people reported in town that Padre Pio was boorish. The poor, the needy, those who mourned their losses in the war, reported instead that he was friendly in his compassion. Sick people who came to meet Padre Pio after doctors had failed to cure them would say, "Padre Pio abrupt? Not at all. He has a patience that never ends." The poor insisted, "Padre Pio loves everybody."

The whole region was poor. The monks were poor too, but just the same when Padre Pio's war pension began to arrive, he refused it. He would not sign the receipt for it, repeating what he had said to the military, "I have done nothing, so why should I take it?"

The friars heard him out in silence. Then they asked him to take the money. He could sign his pension over to the poor, they pointed out. On this understanding, he signed, and at once San Giovanni Rotondo learned that the poor could now count on his war pension.

More and more people came to hear his Mass and to be confessed by him. Padre Pio began to spend three and four hours a day in the confessional. He was especially tender toward the sick, saying that a man in pain was Christ Himself. So an increasing number of sick people made their way up the trail. For them, he prayed long hours during the night in the chapel, by candlelight, looking up at the crucified Christ through his tears.

His long fasting worried the friars. Every few hours, one or the other of the six monks would go quietly to the chapel to make sure he was all right. They moved silently coming and going in their sandals, careful to make no sound so they would not disturb his praying.

Now every Sunday, starting early, a small crowd stood gathered in the clearing in front of the church and monastery. One Sunday in July a murmur suddenly rose in the small crowd. People were turning toward a man they all recognized.

He was Count Luigi Cadorna, who since 1911 had been Army Commander. His troops had been worn out in the Libyan war that went on from 1911 to 1914. He had led his men in eleven battles against Austrian troops, but when Italian soldiers were pushed back at Caporetto he was held responsible for the defeat. The Caporetto disaster had affected him so that his spirit had come close to collapse.

In the clearing of Saint Mary of the Graces, in the midst of the women waiting in line to enter the confessional, the general was looking for a monk to lead him to Padre Pio, whose fame as a "friar of great piety" had reached him in Rome. He met Brother Ferdinando, the eldest of the six, and said, "I wish to talk with Padre Pio."

"Later."

"But at least let me see where he is."

"In the confessional."

"When may I talk with him?"

"Later."

"When exactly?"

"Confessions will be over soon."

The General, in civilian clothes, was allowed to enter the monastery, where he sat on the bench facing the window-counter of the doorman-monk. Before leaving him there, Brother Ferdinando said, "Watch the *clausura*. Padre Pio will be coming that way."

When Padre Pio appeared in the *clausura*, General Cadorna stopped him. "Let me take a good look at you," he said. "I recognize you. Yes. It is incredible. But you are the monk."

With a kindly smile, Padre Pio said, "You took such a long trip just to come and see me?"

"Just to come and see you? You saved my life."

Padre Pio said nothing. He looked at the General for a long moment. Then, still smiling, he nodded good-by and went on through the room, passed through the door, and closed it behind him.

Suddenly breathing hard in a rush of emotion, General Cadorna spoke to the friars and all the faithful in the *clausura*.

"I came here to see if Padre Pio is the same monk who came to
me at a moment when I needed God to help me the most."

One night at the front, he related, after a battle which had
pushed his troops back and had left the battlefield heaped with
casualites, he had retired to his tent, giving orders to the
sentries that for no reason whatever should he be disturbed.
In the tent, he decided to shoot himself. At the moment when
the pistol was in his hand and the hand lifted to his head, a
friar entered the tent. The monk stood motionless, then pronounced these words: "Such an action is foolish."

The monk had saved his life. But where had he come from?
The General asked all the sentries, to whom he had given
specific orders not to let anyone interfere with his privacy.
The answer of all the sentries was the same. Nobody had
passed. And they could assure him that no monk had entered
his tent.

General Cadorna knew he had been visited by a monk, and
that the monk had spoken to him and had caused him to drop
his pistol. "A monk surely came and saved my life. I wanted
to shoot myself," he admitted. When they continued to deny
having seen the friar, the General resolved, "I will find him.
Only if I never find him will I say that I had a hallucination."

Now, at San Giovanni Rotondo, General Cadorna had
found him. Yet how could it be? Padre Pio had been to no
battlefields. No matter. The General insisted that a monk had
come to him in his tent at the front, and Padre Pio was that
monk.

The defeat of Caporetto notwithstanding, General Cadorna
was the field commander best acquainted with the various

efforts of the Allied armies. When the army defeated the enemy on Italian territory, Italy made him Army Marshal. Later he was sent with the military delegation to Versailles to participate in planning the peace treaty. He was a plainspoken man, and he never retracted his affirmation that Padre Pio had visited him in his tent at the front. When reporters, who heard of his story, interviewed him, he could suggest only one explanation. Obviously, Padre Pio had the power to be in more than one place at once.

Many people read the story in doubt, but others, among them veterans who respected the General, believed him. With their brides and children they visited the convent, coming to see the marvelous Padre Pio. To these men, who a moment ago had heard the scream of guns, had sunk a bayonet in the body of the enemy, had felt the blood of companions on their own hands, the three-hour Mass of Padre Pio was a live blessing. If it had been too long for the harried farmers of Pietrelcina, for the veterans it was not long at all. It was the Mass they wanted. To him came the crippled and maimed, and he prayed with them and for them.

Throughout the centuries, Italy had been visited by many a crushing disaster. By sheer power of repetition, the country was resigned to having its men crippled, and to seeing the maimed in its streets. They behaved as if these human beings had their arms and were not blind and did not use a board and wheels to move about.

In vast numbers they came to Padre Pio. What sins had they to confess? In nightmares every night, they relived the terrifying moment when they had ended the life of another human being, and in the confessional they put their recurrent dreams into words. And there were the women, alone and still waiting for their dear ones. There were the women who would wait forever.

Padre Pio saw the same suffering he had seen of old, in Pietrelcina, grown like a malignant tumor. From the window of his cell he saw the land that fed them, or rather had never quite fed the people of the South. He saw the moving line of black-clad women, laboring up the twisted mountain trail. He prayed for each one of them.

Behind the altar he spoke to the Lord of his land and its people. What he had to say to God seemed to have no end. He had been up while the clear moonlight still illuminated his cell. He had left his bed to dress in the light of the sky, had poured water from the jar into the tin basin to wash his hands and face, had passed silently through the short corridor, down the stone stairway. He had crossed the dark rooms by trembling candlelight. Now here behind the altar he knelt, and in full daylight he was still praying. He would always be surprised to see night come again so quickly.

These summer months of 1918 had a sort of loveliness. Hope rose, tenderly, like a new blade of grass. The war was coming to its end, and there was hope that peace would show the dead that they had not died in vain, hope that the new era would prove that tomorrow can be better.

Padre Pio found his own life in these months especially radiant. The Brothers loved him. Every day there were new pilgrims among the faithful coming to Saint Mary of the

Graces. The summer was serene, with no clouds in the sky, and it seemed that the coming fall would be very mild. If so, people would find it easy to keep on coming to Saint Mary of the Graces. It gladdened his heart to baptize the newborn, to perform the ceremony of marriage, to confess, to deliver sermons, to cut away the knots of hatred and sin in the world.

But September came, and on the twentieth of September in 1918, it was all changed.

Chapter 6

As usual, Padre Pio rose in the night and prayed. When the sun came up, illuminating a clear sky, the windows of the second story reflected the blue haze of the sea of Manfredonia in the distance. The light of the sun seemed to bathe the silence of the monastery with something left over of the past summer.

All the Brothers except one occupied themselves with their studies and their prayers. Not Brother Nicola. He was walking to the church and he paused a second at the little door leading behind the altar. He saw Padre Pio kneeling in the shadow, in the dim light of a candle. He went on with his tasks, expecting Padre Pio to rise soon. A little later he returned to the door and looked behind the altar again. Padre Pio was still praying. A second more, perhaps, and then he would rise.

Just how long was a second for a priest kneeling before the Cross of Jesus, bathed in the sweat of death? Brother Nicola made his way silently to the front door of the church, then outside, to the door of the monastery. He took a few steps toward the garden wall.

The silence would have been perfect but for the sudden flight of sparrows into the garden trees. In the clearing there was only the light of the morning sun, and the elm tree offering its little shade. Beyond the clearing, the trail, and the mountains and hills at its sides, had the usual remote, peaceful look.

Brother Nicola re-entered the monastery. He carried in with him the sunlight of a moment ago, and at first he couldn't see into the shadow behind the altar. He paused at the little door, blinking and looking in. Then he froze where he stood. The light was still poor, but he saw, in the trembling candlelight, that Padre Pio had fallen on the floor.

Padre Pio lay half turned, face down. One arm was curled under him, the other spread out in front. Both his hands were bleeding. He lay in a pool of blood, his knees still bent in the position of kneeling, his feet gathered one next to the other, dripping blood onto the hem of the robe.

Brother Nicola leaned over him and put his hands on him. He called him and called again. Then he saw that blood had soaked through the material of his robe from Padre Pio's left side, just below his heart. Padre Pio moaned feebly and tried to move. He opened his eyes and gazed about him. It was a lost gaze, as though he had embarked on a long, long journey and had just returned, and could not recognize anything. Finally his gaze steadied on the face of the Brother who was now kneeling at his side.

The Brother's trembling voice asked, "Tell me, tell me . . ." And he repeated again, "Tell me . . ." He tried to help Padre Pio up and asked, "What is happening to you?"

"Think of yourself," was the answer. As Padre Pio spoke, he moved, made a lurching attempt to rise, failed, tried again and failed once more, his hands slipping on the bloody floor. The Brother helped him to rise to his knees and Padre Pio moved on his knees away from Brother Nicola. He gripped the stalls of the chorus. Then he pulled himself up to his feet. He paused, lowering his head, and brought his bleeding hands up to the level of his chest, over the bloody robe. He looked at his hands, both his palms gleaming with blood in the light of the candle.

Behind him Brother Nicola stood breathless, wavering on his feet, still asking, "What has happened to you?"

Padre Pio took a tentative step, then walked across the room and up the stairway. Brother Nicola stumbled after him. Along the corridor Padre Pio brushed the wall with his shoulder for support. He went on, without slowing his pace, to his cell. He had left a trail of blood behind him. Brother Nicola saw him push open the door, enter the cell, shut the door. There Brother Nicola stood, facing the sign: "The glory of the world has always sadness for a companion." For the moment he could not move. He waited. When he could move he tried to hurry along the corridor, down the stairway. He wanted to go call the Guardian Brother. But in his excitement, when he reached the sacristy he spoke to all the Brothers present.

"Padre Pio is bleeding to death. He is in his cell. I found him in the *coro*, on the floor." He repeated what he had just said as he followed the monks, who were already running up the stairway. At the closed door of cell number five, they stopped. The Guardian Brother entered.

The Brothers gathered by the door, their trembling lips

moving rapidly in prayer. When Father Agostino came out, softly closing the door behind him, they were told to go back to their tasks.

"He is still bleeding," Father Agostino said.

The door of Saint Mary of the Graces was open as always. But the door of the monastery was locked. The doorman-friar locked it early in the afternoon of September 20, after Brother Nicola left for Foggia, the seat of the Provincial Father, and Brother Gaudenzio left for Pietrelcina. In Pietrelcina he spoke only with Don Salvatore.

The archpriest sent for Maria Giuseppe as soon as Brother Gaudenzio stepped out of the rectory. Upon receiving his message, Maria Giuseppe hurried to Saint Mary of the Angels. In the sacristy, Don Salvatore was walking up and down, waiting for her. The look on his face, both worried and happy, puzzled her.

Maria Giuseppe said right away, "Bad news? Is Padre Pio sick again?" Her eyes filled with tears at the thought.

"No," answered Don Salvatore. "No. Maria Giuse," he repeated. "Piuccio has become a saint." He looked firmly into her eyes as he spoke. "It happened yesterday morning," he said. "And this is the way it happened. Piuccio was in the *coro* praying, in the third and last row of the *coro*, where there is a large Crucifix of wood. Piuccio said to Frate Gaudenzio yesterday afternoon that as he prayed he enjoyed a feeling of well-being, a feeling increasing from moment to moment. All at once there was a sharp light, in the *coro*. In that light Christ appeared, said nothing, and vanished. Piuccio fainted.

When he opened his eyes, he was on the floor. He saw that he was bleeding. In his cell he fell on the bed, and he prayed to see Jesus again. Only later, when he was fully conscious, he looked at his wounds and he wept. Piuccio has the stigmata, the same wounds as Jesus Christ."

"But tell me if the pain is too much, tell me if he suffers," she begged, sobbing.

"Piuccio has always suffered, but he takes his suffering and turns it into prayer. Be assured on the condition of his spirit because he says that it is pleasing to the Lord. You are the mother. Remember these words, and be reassured. Tell Orazio to come and see me, let him come at once. Now, come with me, Maria Giuse, let us go into the church and pray."

On the morning of September 23, Padre Pio left his bed. In his cell he wrote a letter to one of his spiritual daughters. The letter, dated San Giovanni Rotondo, September 23, 1918, said: "My very Dear Daughter: Let it be that Jesus is in your heart to fill it to the brim with His holy love. I am sorry not to have the faculty to answer fully all the questions put by you in your letter. I have been infirm for three days. Just now I have left my bed to answer your letter, but forgive me if I am very brief. In general, I can assure you on the condition of my spirit, which is pleasing to the Lord. I cannot believe, as you feel, that you receive nothing from meditation, and therefore I cannot dispense you from meditating. The sacred gift of meditation, my dear daughter, is in the right hand of the Lord. As you empty yourself of burdens, the love of the body and the weight of your will, and learn about holy humility, the Lord will commence to communicate with your heart. Be patient to sustain the exercise of meditation and be content to take small steps at first, until your legs are able to run, or better until you have wings to fly. The reason you cannot meditate, I am sure, is mainly because you begin to meditate with great anxiety, in search of something to gladden your spirit. This is not enough to let you find what you seek. You do not halt your mind in the truth about which you are meditating. My daughter, learn that when one searches with great hurry and avidity something lost, he will touch it with his hands, will see it with his eyes, and still will not be aware of having already found it. The only remedy I know of is to abandon anxiety. The prayers you ask from me you will always have. I bless you with all my soul."

After writing the letter, Padre Pio went down to the chorus to pray, but not for long. It was still early in the morning when he returned to his cell. He was waiting for the Provincial Father, his Regional Superior, who would be followed, during the day, by other authoritative visitors.

A long line from the hierarchy of the order populated Padre Pio's cell for three consecutive days, scrutinized his wounds, touched his garments, the robe wet with blood, his socks, his shoes, watched him bleed. On the morning of the twenty-sixth in a troubled state they left. The Provincial Father left behind orders that Padre Pio's wounds should be photographed and the pictures brought to him in Foggia. He also ordered that, for the moment, Padre Pio should not be available to the general public. He would write a report for the Holy Office in Rome and send the photographs of the bleeding wounds.

When the authoritative visitors had left, Padre Pio went to the *coro* behind the altar and asked the Almighty to give him time to pray. Suddenly time had become scarce.

Early in the morning on September 28, the monks stood at the front door and blinked at the sight of a frightened looking little man, burdened with tripod and boxes and leather straps, out of breath and sweating profusely. "Good morning, I am the photographer," he said. He paused at the door, still holding all his gear.

On the way up the stairway he stumbled on his straps. The monks, right behind him, helped him, picking up the tools he was dropping on the way. Brother Ferdinando, the eldest, knocked on the door of cell number five, entered, then came out and said, "It is all right."

The photographer did not move. "The Father Provincial asked me to do this. As for myself, I do not wish to disturb. I can come back some other time. Any time. Please."

"Well, you are here now, enter," said Brother Ferdinando kindly.

The photographer bowed his head, sweating. He still did not move.

Brother Ferdinando said, "Let us help you carry in your machines. Be at ease, Padre Pio is glad to meet you."

"I am a photographer who has taken all kinds of pictures, but naturally never, never of course . . . and so I am confused and please forgive me."

"Come on in," said Padre Pio from the inside.

The photographer shivered. "Here I am," he said, and he stepped in.

"Sit down on my bed and catch your breath. The pictures will not come out as clear as you want them if you tremble," said Padre Pio. "Nobody is in any hurry, and maybe we should wait a little. Sit now and relax."

"As you wish," stuttered the photographer. "I feel much better already. All my equipment is heavy to carry, that is all. No, it is not. It is the emotion. It is, all at once, like a beautiful day in the winter of my life. My work will be seen by His Holiness the Pope. If you please, Padre Pio, let us take your hands first, secondly the picture of your side, then your feet."

"All right. Here are my hands."

"Put them in the sun, if you will. Like this. Right by the window. Hold it. Perfect. Padre Pio, this will take only a minute."

The monks who had not slept since the twentieth waited in silence along the corridor for the photographer to finish his work and leave. Since the visit of the Provincial Father, they had wondered about his order to keep Padre Pio from the public, whether it could mean that he should be locked in his cell. Would the photographer, although surely a trusted man, keep the secret of the stigmata? Doctors would soon come, and would they keep such a secret? Suddenly it seemed to the Brothers quite incredible that so many people would actually hide a fact which in the long run could not be hidden.

Don Salvatore in Pietrelcina had no such problems. He simply stated to the whole town that Padre Pio had the stig-

mata, that it was the will of God. He thought all the caution
of the monks was nonsense, and that it was even sinful to try
to hide what the Lord was doing. Although he realized the
position of the Brothers, the reasons for the Provincial Father's
wish to delay announcement until doctors had made their re-
ports to the Holy Office, he firmly believed that if the Lord
wanted to keep it all secret, He would not have changed invisible stigmata into visible and bleeding ones.

Don Salvatore's peace was shattered when he met with disbelief.

"What? The stigmata? In 1918?"

"There is no such thing! Absolutely not. There are self-
inflicted wounds, there is hysteria, there is sickness of the mind
which in due time. . . ."

"But never mind that. Do you think it is difficult to show
that monks have terrible secrets?"

"San Francesco D'Assisi? Maybe. That is different. Or I
want to say that I do not mind believing he had them."

"Why, my doctor can tell you without much trouble just
what the matter is."

"This is 1918, not the middle ages. We are living in an en-
lightened world. Padre Pio surely is a good monk, but this we
do not accept. I do not believe in any of these things."

"I say it is hysteria."

"I say the man is mad."

"For my part, I do not believe."

"I do not either and nobody does."

"Nobody does."

"Nobody."

In the barrage of words Don Salvatore regained his peace. The strength of his faith finally found support in the disbelief around him because the many opinions of the doubting began to sound like raving.

He had spoken, believing it fitting that he should speak before gossip and rumors could begin.

On October 9 the first doctor arrived. Dr. Luigi Romanelli of the Barletta civilian clinic was sent by the Provincial Father of the order of the Minor Capuchin Brothers.

Dr. Romanelli carefully visited Padre Pio four times in October and then concluded in his report. "I do not find clinical evidence that would authorize me to classify the five wounds of Padre Pio medically." The report stated that blood was spilling continuously out of the side wound. "It is arterial blood. The side wound is deep," he wrote.

The report was nine hundred words long. It described the wounds in the hands as red membranes with festered capillary tissues, the side wound as shaped like an upside down cross, the foot wounds as larger over the feet, smaller on the bottom. He had pressed with his fingers into the wounds in the palm of Padre Pio's hands and had stopped the pressure at the moment when his fingers were about to go through to the back of the hands. The pressure on Padre Pio's hands was very painful. The back of the hands were equally festered but only slightly bloody, he wrote.

Dr. Romanelli suggested in his report to the Provincial

Father that he thought it advisable to continue his observation over a period of two years. He would visit Padre Pio some five times in that period.

The medical report, together with new copies of the photographs, was sent to the Holy Office by the Provincial Father, who commented that Dr. Romanelli's report was sympathetic toward Padre Pio and very clear professionally.

The next move would be up to the Holy Office.

Instead, the next move came from individual priests in Italy, who attacked Padre Pio in the press. Priests in other Catholic countries defended him and attacked the Italian priests.

The clamor over Padre Pio of Pietrelcina grew so intense that the Brothers, early in 1919, seemed to have been caught in a cross fire. In peaceful San Giovanni Rotondo the monks had nothing less than battle shock to withstand. They did not stand alone, however, for the support for Padre Pio from priests in Ireland, Poland, Spain, France, England grew as quickly as the opposition of priests in Italy. Indeed, even a large number of Italian priests believed that Padre Pio had the stigmata by Divine gift. Among the simple monk's supporters was Pope Benedict XV. "Padre Pio is truly a man of God. He is not appreciated by all as he deserves to be," he said. One day in the spring of 1919, the Pope felt obliged to scold a Bishop who had accused Padre Pio of falsification with the following words, "You are badly informed about Padre Pio, and I order you to go to him to correct your error. Go to San Giovanni Rotondo."

The Bishop's heart was not in the trip he was obliged to take, but he obeyed. When he arrived at the Foggia railroad station, he was approached by two Capuchins from San Giovanni Rotondo, who welcomed him humbly.

"Who told you I was coming?" asked the Bishop in astonishment.

"Padre Pio."

"Padre Pio? But that is impossible! No one knew of this trip, except His Holiness and me."

"Your Excellency, Padre Pio said to us: Go to the station and receive the *Vescovo* who is sent by the Holy Father."

In sudden confusion the Bishop answered, "Well, I am not coming to San Giovanni Rotondo. I am taking the next train back to Rome. The reason is, as you can tell Padre Pio, that if he has been clairvoyant enough to know I was coming, then he knows what I have nourished in my heart against him and the damages I have done to him with my tongue."

Padre Pio's superiors, seeing that the bleeding from the five wounds was persisting and that the attacks against Padre Pio in the press were growing, decided to ask another doctor to visit Padre Pio. They hoped that the new doctor would know how to stop the bleeding, close the wounds, and by doing so, silence Padre Pio's enemies. In July 1919 they asked Professor Amico Bignami, of the pathology department in the University of Rome, to visit Padre Pio and make a report.

In Rome Dr. Bignami learned that to get to the convent of the Capuchins in San Giovanni Rotondo, he would have to travel by horse from San Giovanni Rotondo, the town. He was told there were no accommodations in or around the monastery. The trip up the trail proved to be so fatiguing that when Dr. Bignami reached the monastery he was in an ugly mood. He explained briefly that he had been sent by the Provincial Father to examine Padre Pio at great length.

"Tell me, can you explain why these wounds have appeared where they are and not elsewhere on your body?" he bluntly asked Padre Pio.

"Doctor," answered Padre Pio, "It should be you to tell me why the wounds are where they are, rather than elsewhere." His voice was gentle, his face kindly and smiling as he spoke.

Dr. Bignami did not answer. He cleaned the wounds, put bandages around them, and sealed the bandages with his own marked seal, to be removed when he visited Padre Pio again. He promised that a second visit would take place soon.

In Foggia, where he stayed for a few days, he expressed confidence that Padre Pio's wounds would heal once and for all, and that would be the end of the stigmata. In the days of St. Francis of Assisi it was all different, but in 1919 science had progressed enough medically and psychologically to cope with the problem at hand. He was determined to report "a closed case."

In a few days he returned to the monastery, broke the seals, took off the bandages, and found that the five wounds were still bleeding. He medicated the wounds once more, sealed the new bandages, and departed for Rome.

In his report, he wrote that Padre Pio was "normal, not hysterical." He definitely excluded "a psychopathic case." He was concentrating on "closing the wounds with medicines." In a short time he would visit Padre Pio again, and would medicate him again if the wounds had not healed. He concluded his report by stating that in his examination he had "found Padre Pio in good health, with no trace whatever of his previous lung sickness."

In Rome he insisted that he would "solve the case" in a short time, but by September, 1919, he began to waver. The case of Padre Pio baffled him.

The Holy Office was not satisfied with his report because some of the doctor's anger showed in what he said. Therefore, the Provincial Brother in Foggia was at once instructed to request the opinion of another doctor.

Early in 1920 Dr. Giorgio Festa of Rome came to Padre Pio, arriving much as Dr. Bignami had, with an attitude of skepticism. He examined Padre Pio for a month, seeking a medical classification. Then he called Dr. Romanelli and Dr. Bignami for a consultation, and the three doctors studied the wounds together for fifteen days.

Padre Pio submitted himself to the examinations with docility and patience. When he learned that Dr. Bignami was returning for new visits, without the other two doctors, and then to have a new consultation with the other two doctors, Padre Pio said with a sigh, "But is it really necessary?"

The Brothers bowed their heads and did not answer.

In July, 1920, Dr. Festa declared, "The wounds of Padre Pio never heal." He wrote: "The stigmata are a completely inexplicable phenomenon, if by stigmata is understood the reproduction on the human body of the marks of the crucified Christ. Neither history nor science, nor psychology can afford an explanation."

Before leaving, one by one the three doctors went to say good-by to Padre Pio. As Dr. Bignami was about to leave the cell, he paused. He had just noticed a new element in the case. He closed the door.

"Padre Pio, do you yourself approve of friars using perfume?"

"Perfume?"

"Well, yes. What I mean is, I smell it right here."

Padre Pio closed the window. "Do you still smell perfume?"

"I do. And if you do not mind my saying so, it does not come from the outside, door or window. It comes from you." He took a step closer, "From your clothes, Padre Pio."

"My robe?"

"Sit down on the bed a moment, if you will. I would like to take your bandages off." He took Padre Pio's hands and removed the bandages. "As a matter of fact the odor comes from the bandages. Padre Pio, the smell of perfume is in your wounds. It is your blood that has the odor of perfume. Surely you can smell it. It is pungent. It is very strong and you cannot fail to notice it."

Padre Pio did not answer.

Dr. Bignami said, "Incredible. I can't believe it."

And then Padre Pio answered, "I cannot believe it myself."

"You understand, Padre Pio, I am not very much of a believer, hardly ever think of God. I want to be honest. I am confused. I do not think of God."

"But God thinks of you."

In his professional honesty, Dr. Bignami added in his report that Padre Pio's blood smelled of flowers.

What would the Provincial Office decide to do now? The Brothers, concerned for their brother, soon had further word.

In August, the Provincial Father sent an order of transfer for Padre Pio, who would learn his destination when he arrived in Foggia.

But the people of San Giovanni Rotondo heard of the proposed transfer and, collecting everything they might conceivably use as weapons, gathered at the monastery door, demanding that the friars step outside. The friars filed out to meet them.

"What has happened?" asked the Guardian Brother.

The farm folks lifted their weapons.

"We want to see Padre Pio. A saint is the glory of the country."

The three *carabinieri* and the marshal, outnumbered by far, respectfully suggested that the crowd watch their fire arms, be careful, and calm down. They were answered by the leaders of the swelling population.

"A saint is the glory of the country, alive or dead. Send him to Spain? Not on our dead bodies."

Rather than have Padre Pio leave San Giovanni Rotondo, as it was rumored he was to do, they would kill him and bury his body in Saint Mary of the Graces.

By midmorning more people stood clamoring, armed, angry. They packed the clearing. Armed sentries stood at the doors, along the garden wall and behind the church. The crowd increased during the afternoon. At nightfall the peasants pitched a tent on the monastery grounds. Men on duty guarded all the exits.

The people insisted that the order of departure was for Spain, and in vain the *carabinieri* explained that the monks did not know whether the destination was Spain or somewhere else.

In the morning the people were still there. Padre Pio watched them from his cell, recognizing the mayor of San Giovanni Rotondo, armed like everyone else, and the men and women he had confessed, children he had baptized.

Again the people asked to see the friars and again the friars gathered in front of the monastery. By sending Padre Pio away, reasoned the spokesmen of the crowd, the Franciscan order would prove that foreign countries believed, while Italy, the very place where Padre Pio was born, did not.

"Aside from that," cried the people, impatient of rational argument, "we want Padre Pio to stay right where he is."

They asked that Padre Pio speak to them from the window of his cell. But Padre Pio was not a monk to make speeches from windows. He called to his side one of the least obliging Brothers, Brother Valenzano, a friar whose arms were as strong as his faith. Brother Valenzano, with two other monks, had come from Foggia to help in the crisis. With this staunch monk at his side, Padre Pio walked down to the door to face the people.

The people begged, "You cannot leave us. You are the glory of our country."

By lifting his hands, Padre Pio quieted them. He spoke a few words. "I am not going anywhere. I stay here."

With Brother Valenzano following him, he returned to the monastery.

Now the people could take their tents and return home. But they did not move. It was a brooding crowd. They would make sure that the order to leave, destination Spain, was taken back by the Provincial Father. Only when they were positive that this had happened would they go home.

The people of San Giovanni Rotondo had their way. Because of the demonstration, the order to leave was revoked.

Then the people took their tents and returned home. For another week they came now and then to look things over and make sure no new plot was under way. But eventually they were satisfied. Then the usual peaceful stillness returned to engulf the monastery.

Chapter 7

THE PEOPLE had kept their saint but they soon learned that he could no longer serve them as a priest. Although Padre Pio was still in the monastery, a great change took place before Christmas in 1920. His superiors forbade him to confess, baptize, or perform the marriage ceremony. He was not allowed outside the monastery to visit the sick, to deliver the last rites to the dying, or to perform any of the other pastoral tasks for which he was sought.

These restrictions remained in force for three years. On January 22, 1922, Pope Benedict XV, who had espoused Padre Pio's cause almost from the beginning, died. The new pope, Pius XI, faced with the bitter opposition that had grown up against the extraordinary monk, restricted Padre Pio even further. Padre Pio was to cross himself out, not to be seen and not to be heard. In the impossibility of living constantly in his cell, Padre Pio moved his bed to the library of the convent, which at least was a larger room.

Five years after the appearance of the stigmata, Padre Pio found himself alone, not as a monk would be in a convent, not as Franciscan friars wanted to be throughout the centuries, but utterly isolated. His hands were kept bandaged and covered with half gloves, his feet hidden in the hemp of the ample robe. He had to tread the shadows of empty rooms even when he was on his way to the chapel, and was allowed to say Mass only by himself, in perfect solitude from other human beings. In the early hours of the morning he would steal silently to the chapel of the friars on the second floor, celebrate his Mass, and return to his quarters in the library, without addressing anyone.

Yet his enemies, some of whom were well known priests, were not satisfied. Agostino Gemelli, Franciscan Father, psychologist, newspaper editor, and politician, was one of Padre Pio's most bitter critics. Father Gemelli published in his newspaper a story to the effect that he had gone from Rome, where he lived, to San Giovanni Rotondo to visit Padre Pio. He had asked to see the monk's wounds, and had been refused. From then on he considered Padre Pio a personal enemy, and persecuted him unyieldingly. His campaign of denigration in the press started a series of polemical battles between orders. Father Gemelli maintained that stigmated individuals were hysterical. English Jesuits promptly replied that in that case, the Holy Church had put up two hundred fifty hysterical people as wrong saints, and that therefore, two hundred fifty canonizations had been wrong. But Father Gemelli was not to be silenced so easily.

His attacks not only continued, they became more fierce. He was one of those who persistently demanded that additional measures, over and above restriction, be employed against Padre Pio. "Additional measures" meant only one thing: that he should be divested of the habit of a priest. Once that was done, his enemies wanted the Franciscan Brothers to expel him from the order. But Achille Ratti, Pope Pius XI, would not agree to "additional measure," feeling that restriction alone was justified and sufficient.

Some time passed before the controversy quieted down. Then the shadows closed in, and a complete silence fell about the figure of Padre Pio. He lived day and night in the monastery library, fasted and prayed long, and from his window, watched the brooding mountain. Silence. It was like the silence of the fields when they are shrouded in heavy snow. But there were seeds beneath the snow.

On July 20, 1921, at two-thirty in the afternoon, Monsignor D'Indico of Florence, sat at his desk in his study. In sorrow, he waited for a priest to step out of his sister's room. The last rite was being performed, for his sister was dying of tuberculosis. The door of the dying woman's room opened. Padre Pio stepped out.

He said to the Monsignor, "Have no fear. Tomorrow her fever will be gone, and in a few days she will be healthy again."

Monsignor D'Indico rushed into his sister's bedroom, believing that he was suffering some sort of hallucination. He said to the dying woman and to the priest seated at her bedside, "I have seen Padre Pio."

His sister sat up in bed to say, "Yes, Padre Pio was here. And I asked him: 'Then it is true that you are a saint,' and he answered me: 'I am a person through whom the Lord serves

Himself for His mercy.' Padre Pio showed me his hands, and I kissed his hands."

The Monsignor turned to the priest. "Have you seen Padre Pio?"

"No."

"You are sure?" D'Indico asked. "I have seen Padre Pio. My sister has seen him, and talked to him, and kissed his hands. Have both of us been under hallucination, and at the same time?"

"I am sure I have not seen him. I have been sitting here all along. There has been no one except your sister and me. But what does it matter? Look at your sister. She is sitting up in bed. Only a minute ago, under my very eyes, she was in coma," said the priest.

In Foggia lived a creature that, to move from place to place, had to crawl on its hands and knees. It rolled through the streets of the little town like a barrel, a wooden waterbarrel with loose clamps. Frightened children threw stones at it. Older folks turned their eyes toward heaven and prayed for mercy. It was a boy nine years old, born a hunchback. His spine curved in such a way that his chin seemed pinned to the ground. His name was Giovannino. Every morning he would roll out of bed and over to the basin, splash water and dry himself, and call his mother to dress him. Then he would roll toward the front door.

Every morning, summer or winter, his father said, "Do not let him out. It breaks my heart."

And every morning, winter or summer, the mother answered, "Maybe God will see him today. Let him out."

To Giovannino, it made no difference whether it was summer, winter, spring, or fall. Always, in his heart, it was winter.

One day, when it was indeed winter, as Giovannino crawled in his grotesque, rolling manner over the streets of Foggia, his hands and his knees pressing against the cold ground, he felt something touch his back. Startled, he moved suddenly, and to his astonishment, he found himself standing bolt upright. Then he saw, fleetingly, the bleeding hand that had touched him.

"Padre Pio!" he cried, "Padre Pio!"

But the monk was gone.

And Giovannino ran home, leaping like a yearling.

"Look, I am up," he cried, again and again.

At the door of his own house, his mother greeted him. "What do you want?" she asked formally.

"I am Giovannino, your son! I rose, I rose!"

Then she recognized him, and she fell on her knees.

"Padre Pio raised me."

As though deaf, the mother prayed on in silence.

"Padre Pio touched me with his hands," Giovannino repeated.

The mother leaped to her feet. She ran to the neighbors.

At once the boy was taken to a doctor, and then to other doctors. The doctors examined him carefully and soberly. Their report said that, although Giovannino's heart, and his lungs still slanted in the original position of the hunchback, his spine had straightened out.

Straight as a rod, Giovannino began a pilgrimage from Foggia, leading family, neighbors, and friends, and strangers who also believed to San Giovanni Rotondo. Some of the women made the pilgrimage on their knees, others barefoot and with bleeding feet. The people reached the long mountain trail, then the top of the mountain, then the clearing with the elm tree. But there they stopped before the shut doors, shut windows.

"Here is Giovannino. Here he is. He wants to see Padre Pio. He has come to say thanks."

The mountain answered with echoes of their voices. Then the old perfect silence returned.

The boy, not rolling any longer like a barrel but walking like a human being, returned periodically all by himself. He would ride in a wagon which would give him a lift to the town of San Giovanni Rotondo, and walk on from there. At the end of the trail, he would stand in the clearing and look up at the bell tower. Seemingly tireless, he passed whole days on the grounds of the convent as though it were his home. At the sound of a door opening, he would casually move out of sight. He was not hiding. But he had no need to speak to the Brothers. He simply needed to gratify his longing to be there. But in time, as he returned again and again, the Brothers inevitably came to notice him. His modesty and selfless humility pleased them, and they allowed him to enter the monastery. He did not, of course, see Padre Pio. But he delighted in seeing the convent that housed his benefactor, the little cell where Padre Pio had lived until, upon his seclusion, he had moved to the library. Giovannino haunted the corridor on the second story, and eventually he knew by heart all the signs on the cell doors.

"If you know how to be quiet and how to suffer, you will see how surely God will help you."

"All is vanity except to love God and serve Him alone."

"Hope with all your heart in the Lord, and never lean on your own caution."

"My son, do not reject the corrections of the Lord and do not be impatient when He punishes you."

"Who loves danger will fall into danger."

"The wise man fears and avoids evil, while the fool goes on and knows little fear."

"The Cross is always ready and will wait for you everywhere."

"Close the door behind you and call God."

"My son, while you step closer to the Lord prepare your soul against temptation."

Giovannino repeated the signs along the trail, recited them to people on his way to Foggia and then back again on his way to the convent.

If Padre Pio had been born in Venice, the community around him would have embroidered his works in gold. Perhaps a cathedral would have been erected, to stand where his church stood. Had he been born in Tuscany, and lived in a monastery like the Certosa, the honor accorded him would have taken the form of mystical fascination. But the people of the South were not rich, nor were they sophisticated. They could offer only what they had themselves, and that was a deep, human compassion, born of their own all too broad experience of suffering.

The people said, "Poor Padre Pio."

They did not like the restrictions imposed on him. In sorrow, they raised their voices against his total seclusion.

"What has he done that is wrong?" they said.

And they said, "Must a saint suffer everything?"

But no matter how they complained, there was no response. The people bowed their heads, reasoning that Pope Pius XI knew what was best, and how to protect a man of God from harm.

Unable to do more, they sadly contented themselves with the fact that Padre Pio was there, in San Giovanni Rotondo. They were proud of the revolt they had made to keep him there, for its justification was not fanaticism but bare need. They reasoned that they had been right. In fact the hunchback could now walk. Was not this a reward for them? It was, indeed.

Presently the Brothers needed all the patience they could command. It took steady nerves for them to hold the door shut, while in the clearing gathered the sick, the crippled, the blind. The pilgrims knew that Padre Pio could neither confess them nor celebrate Mass for them, that he could no longer greet them in the little courtyard, nor talk with them at leisure in the shade of the one elm tree. And yet they came. Friars with less than heroic endurance could not have lasted.

Knowing the unpredictable temper of the people of the South, the nine monks were constantly alert. They had seen the peasants armed and angry at the time of the demonstration, and they kept constant watch, like seamen in a storm. They cared for Padre Pio, in his solitude, with love and wonder. And they turned away in sorrow when they were told that a doctor in the town of San Giovanni Rotondo called their charge a sick man, a madman, and worse—a fake. It was Dr. Ricciardi who made such remarks, and he made them to everyone. He was a hardheaded scientific thinker, and he hated to have people singing the praises of a miracle worker. He believed in no miracle workers. "Monks are smart and full of tricks," snapped Dr. Ricciardi, and the credulity of the townspeople angered him.

One day Dr. Ricciardi awakened to find himself astonishingly helpless. He could not rise from bed. Immediately he summoned two colleagues, Dr. Merla and Dr. Juva. Both told him he had a brain tumor. In a matter of days, they predicted, he would die. Calmly Dr. Ricciardi relayed the appalling news to his relatives. With a brain tumor, he told them, nothing could save him. He had been a student of the famous Professor Lombroso, and had earned his medical degree when such degrees were hard to gain. He knew thoroughly the medical facts of his case, and he was convinced that a brain tumor meant death.

"Since you say there is nothing to be done for your body," his family said, "what about your soul?"

"I will throw out any priest you bring here. I am a man of science. Do not put me in the hands of fakes. I beg of you, let me die in peace. I am afraid you are going to mention Padre Pio."

"Perhaps he could comfort you, although we do not say there would be a miracle."

"Good thing he is under restriction."

"Yes," the family said sadly, "he is under restriction. But we could summon another priest."

"Absolutely not."

The family waited. When he ceased to recognize them, they decided to disregard his objections and call a priest.

They found the door of the church closed.

Doors of all churches were closed, and all church bells had stopped ringing. The silence had been ordered by Pope Pius XI, and would last until he succeeded in bringing about a reconciliation between the government of Italy and the Vatican. The dispute between Church and State had been going on since 1859, when Garibaldi's troops had seized Rome. The Pope, then Pius IX, had withdrawn to the Vatican. Every Pope since that time had lived in self-imposed imprisonment in Vatican City. Throughout the sixty long years, four Popes had struggled with successive Italian governments for status independent of the Italian government. The Pontiff of the Church, they argued, should be a citizen of no country, a subject of no king. He should be the first citizen of a *sui generis* state, a free sovereign in his own territory. Vatican City was to be the name of the state, and it should be defined in a political treaty between the Holy See and Italy. St. Peter's Square would be left open to the general public, and the Italian police, but the rest of the territory would be free from the authority of the Italian government or any other government. The only authority was to be the Pope.

Under the name of Lateran Pacts, the treaty was drawn on February 11, 1929. But there were still obstacles, and in July of that year, the treaty had not yet been signed. And so, Pope Pius XI ordered the churches of Italy closed, their bells silenced.

All the churches in Italy, suddenly, had become as quiet as the monastery of San Giovanni Rotondo. People all over the country trembled at such a silence. How many days would it last? Would it last one, two, three days? Would it last a whole month? The people went into mourning.

But after three days of the terrifying silence, the treaty was signed. Churches were opened again, and church bells rang long in celebration.

On July 28, 1929, a priest prayed in the Vatican. His name was Father Luigi Orione, and he was a saintly man. As he knelt in prayer in the semidark of the Vatican Grotte, he saw the figure of a Capuchin monk, kneeling on the tomb of Pope Sarto. It was Padre Pio. The good priest Don Luigi Orione waited until Padre Pio had finished praying, and then stepped up and greeted him. No more than a few words were spoken, yet Don Orione was moved to tears. He stepped aside to let Padre Pio pass, then followed the monk with his eyes, out of the Vatican Grotte and away. As soon as Padre Pio was out of sight, Don Luigi Orione went to Pope Pius XI.

"But how can it be? Is he not in his convent in San Giovanni Rotondo? He is under restriction in the monastery."

Don Luigi Orione answered, "Certainly he is there. He has never moved from there."

Pope Pius XI stretched out his arms. "If you tell me so, Don Orione, it must be so. I believe you. In this case, what good are restrictions?"

Padre Pio was free.

The people of San Giovanni Rotondo formed long lines in front of the church of Saint Mary of the Graces. One by one they stepped up to Padre Pio to say: "We have waited for this day many years." Then each stepped on to let the next person say a few happy words. In town the people spoke of nothing but this event. While the people stood gathered in the square, discussing Padre Pio's suffering during his years of restriction, the monks gathered in their chapel on the second floor to thank God for his freedom.

Now, Padre Pio could go to the dying. While the monks knelt in their chapel, Padre Pio took the holy oils and passed through the monastery door out onto the path leading down the mountain to the town of San Giovanni Rotondo.

He stood, framed in the doorway, on the threshhold of Dr. Ricciardi's bedroom.

"Who has called you, who has called you?" moaned the dying man.

Padre Pio stepped to the doctor's bedside, holy oils in hand. "Peace to this house and to those who inhabit it. Enter, Oh Lord, together with us, and with our humble entrance let come in everlasting happiness, Divine prosperity, joy, and fruitful charity. Let the demons run out. Let the angels come," Padre Pio spoke in Latin. Then he asked, "Do you accept from me the holy oil?"

Dr. Ricciardi reached out and gripped Padre Pio's hands,

oblivious at the moment to their wounds. A cry sounded from Padre Pio's lips.

"I accept," said Dr. Ricciardi.

In the presence of the doctor's family, Padre Pio said, "Your soul is right, and in a few days your body too will be right again."

Dr. Ricciardi, in good health, entered Saint Mary of the Graces for the Christmas Mass of 1929.

Chapter 8

THE MONASTERY at San Giovanni Rotondo was built in 1600. At that time, there happened to be, in the town below the convent grounds, a man named Camillo De Lellis. All his life he had been a vagrant, a tumbleweed, drifting about without home or job, living on the charity of the country. But when he arrived at San Giovanni Rotondo, the monks were at work building their convent. They were kind to Camillo De Lellis, and he responded to their kindness by helping in the construction of the monastery. He proved to be a good mason, and was proud of the work he did for the monks. When it was finished he built himself a house of one room, within sight of the monastery and the good Brothers who were his friends. However, once the monastery was completed, he had no work. For the rest of his life, Camillo lived on the charity of the monks. Thus, it became a tradition for San Giovanni Rotondo to give people in need a pillow on which to rest their heads.

Padre Pio, free after eight years of total restriction, began at once to put to use some money that had been given him. His first project was to widen the trail of San Giovanni Rotondo into a road, so that people who, like Camillo De Lellis, wished to settle in San Giovanni Rotondo, could speedily bring up construction materials.

An American woman, Mary Pyle, was one of the first to build a house and establish herself close to the monastery. Mary Pyle was a psychologist by profession. She had been a collaborator of the well known Italian psychology professor, Dr. Montessori. She had lived in comfortable circumstances all her life, and after she had provided for her retirement at San Giovanni Rotondo, she donated what remained of her money to the people of Pietrelcina, to build a church. The church was built, exactly as Padre Pio had wished in his early youth.

When, in the December frost and winds, Maria Giuseppe Forgione arrived at San Giovanni Rotondo to attend her son's Christmas Mass, Mary Pyle immediately invited her to stay at her new house. Maria Giuseppe accepted with deep gratitude, for the trip from Pietrelcina had exhausted her, and the biting weather had chilled her to the bone. The little church of Saint Mary of the Graces, packed with people, grew very warm during the lengthy Christmas Mass. After the services, when the worshippers stepped out of the church into the raw mountain air, the cold seemed more intense than ever. Maria Giuseppe, not yet recovered from the fatigue of her journey, caught a severe cold. In a few days, she was running a high fever. Mary Pyle nursed her tenderly, but her efforts were of little use. Maria Giuseppe's condition was soon critical.

Said Dr. Ricciardi, "Padre Pio took care of me. Six months ago I was dying. All will be well with Maria Giuseppe. Padre Pio will pray for her recovery."

The people of San Giovanni Rotondo hoped that the doctor

would prove to be right, but when they saw the faces of Dr. Merla and Dr. Juva when they stepped out of Mary Pyle's house, they feared that Dr. Ricciardi, who had been wrong once, was wrong again.

Padre Pio prayed long at his mother's bedside. Often he wept. Once he said, "At times the Lord lets you feel the weight of the Cross. It seems unbearable, but you carry it because the Lord, in His love, gives you the strength to carry such a weight." His mother, conscious despite her critical state, heard the words, and looked at her weeping son with selfless maternal compassion. It grieved her that she should grieve him.

Padre Pio visited her every day during her brief illness, kneeling for hours at her bedside.

The people clustered about Mary Pyle's door. They heard Padre Pio lament at Maria Giuseppe's bedside. He wept over the yesterdays of Pietrelcina, the rains and the snows and the mud of old, frosted mornings and those bewildering nights, the long hot summers, the hungry winters, the woman herself always enduring.

Orazio was sent for, and arrived while his wife still lived. But before long, Maria Giuseppe's hands let the rosary rest on the border of the bedsheet.

Four pallbearers carried Maria Giuseppe's coffin the short distance from Mary Pyle's house to Saint Mary of the Graces. A soft, gentle snow began to fall. On the way to the cemetery after the Requiem Mass, the snow fell a little harder. Big, soft snowflakes settled lazily on the coffin and on the black garb of the mourners, and there they clung.

Maria Giuseppe was buried under the eyes of a host of

people, old friends and new ones. Old friends laid flowers on her grave. New friends prayed for her.

Among the mourners gathered around the plot in the snow were many who believed the dead woman's son, through his intercession, had cured them of afflictions.

Maria Cozzi Giuliana, of Ghizzano, in the province of Pisa, had been cured of epithelioma in August of 1919. For seven months her tongue had been swollen with fungus. Doctors had told her that surgery would be difficult, but that she should try it. She agreed, and arranged a date to enter the hospital for the operation. Before the day came, she mentioned the impending ordeal to a priest, who had heard the remarkable stories about Padre Pio and believed. The priest gave her a picture of Padre Pio, and told her to visit him and ask him to pray for her. She did as the priest suggested. A few days later, she was bothered by a toothache and went to her dentist. He found a minor infection at the aching tooth, but saw that her tongue was perfectly normal. Greatly surprised, he took Maria to Dr. Marchetti at the hospital, to see if he could explain the cure. Dr. Marchetti could not explain, but he confirmed the dentist's findings. The disease had vanished.

A young man of seventeen stood among the mourners at Maria Giuseppe's grave. In the crowd of humble peasants, he stood out, for his bearing and manner marked him at once an aristocrat. His father was Count Marzotta of Florence. For nine years, since 1916, the boy had enjoyed the fruits of Padre Pio's intercession.

As a young child, he had had such severe trouble with his eyes that, by the time he was eight years old, he was nearly blind. It happened that the colonel of the San Giovanni Rotondo *carabinieri*, a man named Paranelli, was acquainted with the boy's family, and the child's condition seemed to him pitiable. One day, he mentioned it to his friend, lawyer Bramante, who also lived in San Giovanni Rotondo and knew Padre Pio. Paranelli asked Bramante if he would mind calling the boy to Padre Pio's attention, and Bramante readily agreed to do so. When Count Marzotta heard from Paranelli of this plan he eagerly brought his son from Florence to San Giovanni Rotondo to see Padre Pio. The priest greeted them with his customary warmth. "Let us pray together to the Lord," he said. After four days, the boy could see without the thick glasses he had been required to wear.

On Easter Sunday in 1925, Paolina Preziosi, mother of five children, lay dying. Doctors had diagnosed her illness as double pneumonia. They had also pronounced the case hopeless. The husband of the dying woman, although he knew that Padre Pio was at that time under restriction, went to the monastery to plead for his intercession. He spoke with the doorman-monk, and begged him to give Padre Pio a message about his wife's crisis. The message was delivered, and the doorman-monk brought Padre Pio's reply to the worried husband. "Do not fear, because when tomorrow the bells ring, your wife will be well again." And now, in 1929, Paolina Preziosi stood praying at the grave of Maria Giuseppe Forgione.

Another of the mourners was a Dr. Morelli, professor at the Montevideo, Uruguay, medical school. He, too, had good reason to believe in the efficacy of Padre Pio's prayers. Years ago, just before total restrictions had been imposed on Padre Pio, he had witnessed an event so extraordinary as to deserve the name of "miracle."

A patient of his, Mother Teresa Salvadores, Superior of the Catholic Taller Madella Milgrosa Academy of Montevideo, came to him suffering from stomach cancer. Dr. Morelli could do nothing. He knew there was no hope.

Sadly, he watched his patient's strength decline as the disease progressed. For long, agonizing months, her suffering grew more and more intense. During those months, a Monsignor Damiani, who was a friend of Mother Teresa Salvadores', paid a visit to Italy. Having heard of Padre Pio, he went to the little monastery at San Giovanni Rotondo, begged Padre Pio to pray for his friend, and obtained from the humble monk-priest one of his gloves—the one that had covered the stigmata of the right hand.

When he returned to Uruguay, he went at once to Mother Teresa Salvadores' bedside, and gave the glove to the nuns caring for the Superior. That night, they applied the glove to the woman's swollen side. As the Sister later related, she had dreamed of Padre Pio, who had spoken to her of God. "Three hours later I awoke and asked for my clothes, and I left the bed which I had not been able to leave for many months. At the noon meal I was in the refectory where I ate more food than all the other Sisters, and from that day on I never felt any pain again."

When these people, who stayed in San Giovanni Rotondo for a few days after Maria Giuseppe's funeral, expressed their gratitude to Padre Pio, he answered, "I have done nothing. Good people, do not involve me. You, with the force of your faith, helped yourselves."

Not long after he was released from the order of solitude and silence, Padre Pio found a new group of sufferers, whose sorrows touched him deeply. This new group owed its existence, and its plight, to the new era. In 1922, when Mussolini had led his Fascist regime to power in the famous "March on Rome," he had promised to revive for Italy the glories of ancient Rome. In order to do so, it appeared, it was necessary to raise new armies, levy new taxes, and assume complete control of the schools and the newspapers, industry and labor. Empire was the aim of the new government, and they would brook no opposition.

The determination of the new leaders to have their way resulted in the creation of a new kind of citizen, the political exile. The little isolated mountain towns of the South became prisons for those who protested the harsh rule of the Fascists. Suddenly there were new faces in San Giovanni Rotondo. A poor farmer from Sicily, a student from Florence, a pharmacist from Lucania, came to the little town to live, far from their homes and families and livelihoods. The government provided five lire a day for them to live on, and required them to report to the police every day. San Giovanni Rotondo did not know what to do with these new people, whose lives had been wrecked. If they befriended the exiles, would they be jeopardizing their own safety? On the other hand, could

Christians treat the unfortunate like lepers? The people of San Giovanni Rotondo were unhappy.

Now, when a new individual appeared in town, they could never tell whether he had come voluntarily to climb to the monastery, or had been sent by the government. Their hearts sank at the sight of a newcomer. If he were another exile, soon San Giovanni Rotondo would no longer merely be a town of banishment, but a true concentration camp for political criminals.

The exiles were expected to live a life of misery away from home. The loneliness and poverty they suffered were supposed to break their spirits. But instead, to the bewilderment of the police, their faces began to show contentment. Singly and in groups, the exiles visited Padre Pio. Early in the morning, they trooped up to the monastery, were confessed, heard Mass, and received the Holy Communion from Padre Pio, and then lingered on the premises of the monastery.

Because the banished were part of the suffering Christian world and had been unjustly deprived of civil freedom, Padre Pio befriended them.

Patiently he conversed with the exiles in the quiet garden, imparting to them his own imperturbable courage, and teaching them the meaning of forgiveness. In the town the exiles were reminded that during his restriction, Padre Pio had been quoted as saying, "Sweet is the hand of the church, even when it seems harsh." Equally now, their native land could be nothing but sweet, even though they had been forced to oppose other Italians.

The banished loved him. Among themselves they ignored the miracles that everywhere were attributed to Padre Pio.

Such delicate matters were the concern only of the supreme authority of the Church, and only the Church could judge. They interested themselves in what they could see. Padre Pio's appearence was that of the most humble of Capuchin friars. Nonetheless, before him came high religious officials, and all were deeply impressed. There was no apparatus around him, nor any elaborate ceremony. Padre Pio could be met in the sacristy or in the monastery like any other of the monks. There was no need of a special introduction to him. To avoid the eyes of the merely curious, he wore half-gloves. During the celebration of the Holy Mass, when his hands were bare, he tried to hide them in the long sleeves of his robe. But inevitably, the wounded hands were visible during certain parts of the ceremony. On his feet he wore black leather shoes, very light, over his bandages, and although he wavered as he walked, this motion was not very noticeable. Finally, the fame of Padre Pio seemed to have spread everywhere. Pilgrims were coming from France, Spain, Poland, Ireland, England, and both Americas in a continuous flow. Letters came to Padre Pio even from China, written in Chinese.

The banished found it easy to bear their burden of exile, when exile meant the friendship of this extraordinary man. Local Fascists were astonished. They informed the government that San Giovanni Rotondo, because of Padre Pio, was not the right place to send people who had clashed with the authority of the state. The exiles in this town felt themselves blessed rather than punished.

Would Padre Pio be subjected to persecution by the Fascists because he was befriending the banished?

On May 5, 1931, *Il Resto del Carlino*, a Bologna daily, published the following article, written by Alberto Spaini. "In the region of the Gargano mountain Padre Pio is called the saintly *Padre*. It is not up to us, of course, to indulge in expressions that might sound like the process of canonization of Padre Pio. On the other hand the manifestations of the extraordinary that surround him are well known. Scientists have discussed the stigmata, which make his hands, side, and feet bleed. They have discussed some of the remarkable benefits received by numerous believers and attributed to Padre Pio's miraculous intervention—cures, and apparitions taking place in times of danger or sorrow. Many pilgrims have been scented with perfume, which comes from his wounds. Many have been momentarily blinded by a light which comes from his face. Pilgrims talk of miracles. Many who have come to insult and offend him have been converted instead. The people of San Giovanni Rotondo talk of the chief of public security who recently came to Padre Pio to warn him not to befriend the exiles. Instead of intimidating Padre Pio, the chief of security was so moved by their meeting that he became a convert himself."

No, the Fascist regime would not persecute Padre Pio. Nor would they stop sending exiles to San Giovanni Rotondo. After all, there were churches in every town and village, and the regime could not possibly find a place without one. Moreover, Rome had meant to deprive the exiles of their civil rights, not their faith.

The exiles were, by and large, dismally poor, but not every visitor to San Giovanni Rotondo suffered poverty. Among the pilgrims were a few who were prosperous, as well as the many who were not. All the pilgrims, rich or poor, wanted to show Padre Pio in some way their appreciation of him, and those who could placed donations in his hands, to be used as he saw fit.

Padre Pio's first move was to call back the laborers who had widened the trail leading to the monastery. This time, they were to build a drainage system on the uphill side of the road and supporting walls on the downhill side. Thus the houses being built close to the monastery would soon be protected against landslides.

At the same time, Padre Pio was working out a more sweeping reconstruction plan designed to bring greater prosperity to San Giovanni Rotondo as a whole. This plan called for the building of a good road from Foggia up the mountain into San Giovanni Rotondo, the town. The construction demanded by this plan was of such magnitude that it would require ten times the sum Padre Pio had to complete the job.

Because of the habitual poverty of the area, taxes could rarely be collected in full. San Giovanni Rotondo township owed a substantial amount in back taxes to the province, which in turn owed money to the state, which had to decide how to pay a tremendous war debt and feed and clothe more Fascist legions at the same time. Yet the tax collectors, who were perpetually harassed by this problem, were among the first to donate money when they saw a group of laborers, provided with makeshift tools, at work near Foggia, and another group digging drainages and erecting supporting walls along the road from the town to the monastery.

Long before, in 1923, Padre Pio had mentioned in a letter to Dr. Merla and Dr. Juva, both of San Giovanni Rotondo, a plan which at that time had been thwarted. "I believe I am waiting in peace for the realization of promises. You speak of institution, and you can imagine how I have always loved the idea, but if Jesus does not give me a little more freedom, and those who hold the place of God do not give me moral support, what can I do? But then, what Jesus wants will be done at its proper time. I am in the hands of Divine piety."

By "institution" Padre Pio meant a hospital on the grounds of the monastery. Even in the fall of 1931, the project could not be undertaken. Restrictions had been lifted, yes, but where could such a large sum of money come from? The institution would have to wait. But meantime there was a more modest plan that could be undertaken. With Padre Pio's support, a free infirmary was opened in the town, for the poor of San Giovanni Rotondo. It was a first step.

In Rome, newspapers commented on these developments. San Giovanni Rotondo *has struck it rich*, the articles said. With one road already built, one in process of construction, and a new infirmary for the poor, the town did indeed seem to be prospering. The press was satisfied. But not Padre Pio.

From everywhere now cripples and invalids arrived. They came in such numbers that one day Padre Pio cried out, "Oh Lord, my Lord, what endless miseries."

A large hospital was needed. But before it could be built the road up from Foggia must be completed. This in itself was a major engineering problem.

San Giovanni Rotondo was not ready for a large hospital.

All this southern town could do, while in Rome the third Italy was building new quarters for the regime, new houses for top Fascists, a new army, was to look back at the roads still existing in Pompeii, still usable. Even centuries of volcano lava had not destroyed them. The ancient remains of the famous town were not far away, so that folks from San Giovanni Rotondo could visit it, and stand in wonder at the beauty and durability of the work of other builders once living in the now empty city.

San Giovanni Rotondo had been left in such a primitive condition over the centuries that now it did not know where to begin. But changes were taking place every day. The people saw new faces each day, and this in itself, for people of a mountain village, opened a wide window on the world. They heard new tongues. Since the last invasion of the South, centuries ago, they had heard nothing but their own dialect.

Not all the people who arrived suffered tumors, epilepsy, leprosy, blindness, and not all had seen a monk in their dreams to change ways leading into perdition. The long line of women on Sunday, for instance, came as they would go to any other church, in holiday spirit if it were a holiday. Most of the people had no great sins to confess, but simply wanted to hear Mass, not making any particular distinction between Saint Mary of the Graces and their home-town churches.

When a crowd gathered, experience suggested to the monks that they should not linger in front of the church or the monastery, especially near the doors, for the crowd might suddenly press forward with little thought for any friar who might be in their path. Experience had proved that, with the women, the monks should insist on discipline and watch them carefully. Otherwise, as it had occasionally happened, they might invade the monastery, and frighten a friar to death by a sudden appearence in his cell.

The friars gradually developed a code of protective devices. Each monk should first of all protect himself, secondly try to protect the others. One monk, for example, would hardly ever furnish information as to the whereabouts of another.

"Where is Frate Nicola?"

"He was here a moment ago. I do not know. Look in the church."

"He is not there, I have looked. I want to see him to be introduced to Padre Pio."

"Have you looked in the garden?"

"There is nobody in the garden."

"Well, wait. He will be back."

"From where?"

"If I knew I would tell you where he is."

In this manner the monks hoped to provide some respite for the friar who could not be found at the moment. Time spent waiting went into prayer, and the other monks would be left free for more pressing problems. On the other hand, those who came to see Padre Pio in emergencies, or burdened with overwhelming problems, found the monks sympathetic and helpful.

The Guardian Brother, Padre Agostino, formed the habit of carrying a bamboo cane around with him, rapping men who crowded the Brothers too much and reached for their garments. "Folks, folks, you are in the house of God, please.

Be of good manners, good people." He tapped them with the bamboo. He would not touch the women, but merely waved the cane at them. "Daughters of Eve, daughters of Eve," he would say. One day a Neapolitan woman, who did not care for his derogatory tone, snapped, "Well, let me ask you who was your mother, are you not also the son of Eve?" When Padre Pio was told of her remark, it made him smile.

The nine monks also had all they could do to make sure none brought injury to the premises, for the crowds of visitors wanted to have tokens, relics, material proofs of their visit to the convent of Padre Pio. Despite their vigilance, one day the bench in the ground-floor corridor, opposite the window-counter of the doorman-monk, disappeared. The Brothers stood staring at the spot where the solid wooden bench had stood for years. After all, it was a heavy bench. But the Brothers had not nailed it down.

"It seems impossible."

A layman standing nearby commented, "The statues on the Via Appia in Rome would vanish if they were not nailed down. I can just see where it is, on a farm, under the shade of a tree. An old man about to die is sitting on it, and what can gladden his heart more than to sit all afternoon on 'the bench of Padre Pio'?"

The Brothers looked at him and saw his own description incarnated. He was a farmer, old, obviously rapidly fading. But they said nothing. It seemed incredible that he would have had the strength.

At first, the Brothers had hoped that the crowds would somehow slow down, at least one day a week. But as the weeks passed and the number of visitors increased instead of decreasing, they became resigned. But then they were even more alert, skillful, and enduring.

"Brother Gaudenzio?"

"Yes."

"I come from Milano."

"A long trip."

"I am very lucky to have found a room in San Giovanni Rotondo these last four days."

"I am glad for you. Has the room been expensive?"

"Expensive? Brother Gaudenzio, let me tell you this. Perhaps there are no people on earth as poor as the people of San Giovanni Rotondo. Yet I am charged the price of a pack of cigarettes. The same it is happening about food. Four days here I have been saving money. It would be the most natural thing for them to get rich now, quickly. All they would have to do is charge a normal rate for a room, a normal price for food and wine. That would do it. And they do not do it."

"Good, good," Brother Gaudenzio answered, beaming. "Good-by now, and good fortune."

Not all the pilgrims were fortunate enough to find rooms in the little town. Often a number of those who wished to stay overnight could not be accommodated. Of these, many were women. As the sun went down, they would gather sadly in the clearing before the monastery wondering what to do.

In the evening, before too long, a tall, stout woman with rosy cheeks and a cheerful, glowing face would greet the women. This was the American woman, Mary Pyle.

"You have not found a place to stay tonight? You are welcome to stay with me." And she would lead them to her house. The Italian women were curious about her. "How come you are here?" With great simplicity she would answer that God had "closed" her here.

By 1934 a group of Tertiary of the Order had settled down around the monastery and Mary Pyle was one of them. They wore the habit of the Franciscan Third Order, a simple Franciscan robe, scapular, sash, and rosary, but no veil. They used a mantilla to cover their heads in Saint Mary of the Graces. They shared one large house erected on the downhill side of the road, its rooms not unlike the cells in the monastery. Their mission was to make pilgrims comfortable, and it was a rare occasion when the house was not filled with people of all nationalities.

Chapter 9

In the middle thirties, Orazio, who had returned to Pietrelcina after Maria Giuseppe's funeral, came to settle permanently in San Giovanni Rotondo, in the house of Mary Pyle. Orazio was seventy-four years old. He was a quiet, kindly man, who, with his dignified manner, the thick tapestry of wrinkles that covered his face, and his natural humility seemed much like a *fratozzo* himself.

Times had changed. "Yes, if I were in America now, I'd be out of work. Just imagine, in America. It is incredible." With Mary Pyle he would speak half in English, half in Italian.

Before dawn, Mary Pyle would walk along the corridor between the cells in her house sounding a little bell. And Orazio would awaken, and be off to his son's Mass.

Orazio was sometimes pleased by what he saw, sometimes sad. The people who visited the monastery had little consideration for Padre Pio. Every day, he was practically nailed into the confessional box from early morning on. If his fate had been completely in the hands of the faithful, Orazio feared, they would have asked Padre Pio to skip even his meal of boiled greens so as to be available to them continuously.

But he was pleased to see that his son, now forty-eight years old, looked much younger than his age. Despite his constant bleeding and his modest diet of greens, Padre Pio was as florid as he had been in his boyhood.

Italy now had law and order. But freedom had vanished, and the order resembled the lineup of a prison compound. To reward people for good behavior, regime and kingdom gave them little decorations, called *cavaliere* ribbons. Thousands of these ribbons were assigned weekly.

In Orazio's presence one day, a man walked up to Padre Pio and asked, "Tell me, are your stigmata painful?"

"They are not *cavaliere* ribbons," answered Padre Pio with a smile.

While the ribbons were being mailed out, a strange economic erosion was taking place. The middle class dropped to the condition of the poor, and the rich were growing richer. When the monks had first made inquiries about the land at both sides of the trail, in order to buy enough to enlarge the trail, the deeds were in the hands of a number of people. Now, just a few years later, half a dozen people owned it all.

Concentrated ownership of land had always been the rule around San Giovanni Rotondo. Great tracts were in the hands of a few gentlemen farmers. But now one man owned five mountains. In the midst of law and order people had lost their property. The very rich invested their money in ammunition factories. In the long, peaceful summer evenings, the factories worked overtime. Why ammunition factories? The answer came in 1935.

The regime put suntan uniforms on its troops and sent them to Africa. Although at first it was understood that the war was to be fought by party militiamen only, now soldiers were being drafted. Men born in 1912 and 1914, most of them already married, were being sent to fight against the barefoot troops of Haile Selassie, Emperor of Ethiopia.

Soon, mothers, brides, fathers, and grandfathers came to weep at Padre Pio's feet.

Alone in the night on his knees, Padre Pio could not restrain his tears in front of the Crucifix. The World War seemed so few years ago, and now, again, men were dying by violence.

The doomed South, which had never ceased to be doomed, poorer now and suffering more than before the World War, gathered the casualty telegrams and turned to Padre Pio. He prayed for the whole South as the South prayed for itself. In Saint Mary of the Graces, Padre Pio and the people appealed to God, because man did not have anyone else to put trust in. Kneeling behind the stigmated priest, the people felt inwardly changed, "for the word of God is quick, and powerful."

Busy with the manipulation of trusting folks, the regime flexed its muscles. The little people, not understanding the mystique of the government, the promises and ranting of the black-shirted orators, had stepped closer to their priests, who spoke a language two thousand years old.

Now the little people would stop any of the monks and would ask, "But who wants an empire? Do you?"

At the League of Nations, it appeared, sanctions would soon be approved against Italy. War casualties grew. The regime had promised that the Ethiopian campaign would be a simple affair, lasting for a few months. But now, people began to fear complications. Possibly there would be a world war.

Padre Pio was now completely absorbed by the total burden, the suffering caused by the war and the complications that might develop. In his own prayers and in his Mass he prayed intently that the living be spared a living hell, that the dead be spared suffering through eternity.

The strain of long hours in the confessional and even longer hours in prayer showed on his face. Orazio, watching his son, was sad. Dr. Giorgio Festa, who early in 1920 had been sent by the Holy Office to make a report on Padre Pio and was now returning periodically to San Giovanni Rotondo as one of Padre Pio's spiritual sons, assured Orazio that Padre Pio was very strong. In 1925, when Padre Pio was under strict restriction, Dr. Festa had operated on him. It was then, the doctor told Orazio, that he had realized how strong Padre Pio was. The operation, for the removal of hernia, had lasted two hours, and Padre Pio had not accepted any anesthesia. Everyone in the operating room had seen Padre Pio's bleeding side, his bleeding feet. While he was on the operating table, Padre Pio had turned to his friend Dr. Juva, who was assisting Dr. Festa, and had said, "As I leave the operating table it is your turn. This is the time for your operation. Have courage and go through with it." Dr. Juva was astonished. It was true that he had been postponing an operation he needed for many months.

Padre Pio's own operation was horribly painful. In his agony, his eyes filled with tears, and he murmured, "Lord, forgive me. I have never offered You anything of value, and now that You give me this poor occasion, I lament without reason. This is nothing compared with what You suffered on the Cross. My Lord, forgive me." When surgery was finished, Padre Pio called one of the Brothers to his side and asked, "Let me ask you, do you think that the Lord has accepted this present suffering for a little relief to . . ." and he mentioned the name of a man who had asked Padre Pio to pray for him.

The campaign in Africa ended and in April, 1936, Italy annexed Ethiopia. As the little people said in San Giovanni Rotondo, this was an empire for the rich, not anything poor people wanted. First of all they did not even know where Ethiopia was. Even if they did learn something about it, it was still the home of the Ethiopians and not their home. They did not wish to intrude in other peoples' affairs. They felt that dropping bombs on defenseless people had been murder, and they wanted nothing to do with such sin.

In the spring of 1936, with the good weather, new crowds, together with the old, populated the clearing in front of Saint Mary of the Graces from early morning to late at night. One day, as the people waited patiently in the long lines before the confessional, they heard Padre Pio's voice rise suddenly.

"You go away," he said to a man who had just knelt to confess himself. "Go away from here. You are planning to murder your wife."

The man broke into tears, rose, and moved away. To the astonished bystanders, he admitted that it was true. In the secret of his heart he had made such a plan while climbing the road to the monastery. Alone, brooding, he had thought to return home and do away with his wife. But now he would

wait in San Giovanni Rotondo until Padre Pio gave him absolution, if he would, because his heart was changed.

Others in the group commented that Padre Pio usually
knew of their sins beforehand. In the confessional he would
ask leading questions, pause, until he was able to elicit the
confession of sins they had not wanted to speak about, or had
no idea how to put into words. Others recounted that Padre
Pio had refused them absolution.

Priests who had visited San Giovanni Rotondo knew of
many instances when Padre Pio had refused absolution. Father
Sabino Cassatella, in the newspaper *La Voce del Parroco* related: "At times Padre Pio refuses the absolution. One who
does not deserve it does not receive it. One evening, as I was
saying the rosary close to Padre Pio, a young man came to
me and asked, 'Tell me what I must do, now that Padre Pio
has refused me the absolution. I must leave before evening. I
would wait if I could, but I cannot wait.' I answered: 'If Padre
Pio denied it to you, be sure that any other priest would have
done the same. Practice what Padre Pio told you, and then
go to your own priest and confess with the determination not
to repeat whatever caused the humiliation imparted on you by
Padre Pio.' The young man said that Padre Pio had read his
heart, and had sent him away because he was not well dis-
posed."

An increasing number of priests, like Father Cassatella,
came to the Gargano Mountain to see Padre Pio. Many came
in hopes of being allowed the privilege of serving Padre Pio's
Mass. Father Gino Frediani, in *La Vita Cattolica* wrote about
his stay in San Giovanni Rotondo. "On Friday morning, at

five o'clock in the morning, we rose and started out in a wind
storm for the convent, walking for about half an hour up the
road. Even at that hour we found Saint Mary of the Graces
full of people. In a few minutes Padre Pio would come down
for the Mass, and therefore all present were trying to pick
places from which they could best see him during the long
sacrifice. I, as a priest, went directly to the space behind the
altar, which was used as sacristy. There I found many other
priests, Brothers, lay-Brothers, all gathered in deep silence,
waiting for Padre Pio. I was new there and I did not know
how to act. I turned to the first Brother I saw and I asked him:
'Is it possible to serve the Mass for Padre Pio?' The answer
was a negative one. Without saying more, I went before the
altar to start the recitation of the prayers. In less than five
minutes, I saw Padre Pio, in the vestments of the Mass. As he
approached the altar, his face was transformed, and as I tried
to step back out of his way, he gave me the great news, saying
to me: 'Reverend, do serve the Holy Mass!' In that moment
of great joy for me, serving his Mass, I saw that he was not
a man along with other men, among other men, but the priest
who, because of singular privileges, relived all the minutes of
the passion of Jesus. Very much alive and visible to all were
his various physical pains, and I believe also moral pain, during
the whole Mass, which lasted over two hours. But during that
whole time none of the congregation moved, so attentive were
they. These people had come from many parts of Italy and
from several foreign countries. All eyes were turned to Padre
Pio, as though fascinated, won by a Divine power, in intimate
union with Padre Pio."

In the winter of 1936, soldiers were still returning from Africa, where all military operations had stopped months before. One day, a veteran on crutches, made his way up the good, well-graveled road. For three days in the harsh December cold, he sat in front of the door of Saint Mary of the Graces. He would leave the clearing only for his meals. For the whole three days, he showed the people coming and going a gash in his knee. His face was bathed in tears. His own wounds were not the only reason for his sorrow. In 1936 the civil war in Spain had just begun, and his brother had gone there to fight with the Nationalists. When he himself had returned from Ethiopia, with his painful, crippling wound, his spirit had been crushed by the news that his brother was reported missing. After his three days of crouching on the church steps in prayer and weeping, he finally steeled himself to go to Padre Pio. The compassionate people moved aside to let him enter the church before his turn. He knelt before Padre Pio as best he could with only one good leg, and Padre Pio motioned to the crowd to give space to the crippled soldier. Then Padre Pio lowered his head toward the man.

"Throw away your crutches!"

"Padre Pio, I cannot. I need them to kneel, to get up. I cannot walk without my crutches."

"Open your hands and let the crutches go. Drop them!"

In the silence of the church the veteran's breathing sounded unnaturally loud. "Padre Pio, I am afraid. I will fall."

Severely, Padre Pio said, "Stand up."

The veteran tried to keep all his weight on his good leg. Still gripping the crutches, he tentatively touched the floor with the crippled leg. Then suddenly he opened both hands and let his crutches go, standing on his two feet as the crutches crashed to the floor. He took a few steps. Then he cried aloud with joy. He could walk, run, leap, his leg was cured. The gasp that rose from the crowd quivered the windowpanes in the church. Padre Pio was already walking away, slightly wavering on his feet as ever, toward the sacristy, behind the altar.

Behind the altar, night after night Padre Pio implored God to relieve the suffering imposed on the Spanish people by their civil war. In the early morning he would resume the massive, strength-consuming labor of praying. Insistently, he repeated the name of the veteran's brother who was missing in Spain. In prayer, as in dealing with the complex fate of a soul, he was detailed, forceful, and appealing. The little people believed with their whole hearts in the efficacy of his prayer.

They spoke of their beliefs to Orazio. The soldier who had thrown aside his crutches remained in the town for three days after the miracle. He would sit peacefully with Orazio, basking in the happiness of being able to run again. Suddenly things which had mattered a great deal in the past seemed small, and he did not fear poverty or unemployment. He was sure his great faith would lead him now along different paths.

"They have told me here," he said, "that when the American woman, Mary Pyle, gave her money to build the church in your home town of Pietrelcina the builders could not find water, and Padre Pio pointed on the map and said: 'Here is the water.' They have told me that now, when there is a dry season in Pietrelcina and the town does not have water, people go to the church for the water, and the priests always have water for the people."

Orazio nodded and smiled. "Yes, they have water."

"Here I am and there is the water, yet there are people who do not believe," said the veteran in sadness.

In Saint Mary of the Graces, just that day, a young man had stopped Padre Pio and had said, "Padre Pio, my friend here does not believe you have the stigmata." He pointed to his friend standing at his side. And Padre Pio had answered with a smile, "Well, I almost do not believe it myself."

But, often, at such assaults, Padre Pio would turn away abruptly. Closed in by a solid crowd, all inching closer to his hands, he would say, "But will you let me through?" and he would stand until they moved. He disliked curiosity just as he dismissed admiration. Pilgrims who came to the priest were favored. Those who had come to see the stigmata were left to themselves, none of the Brothers providing any help.

Padre Pio's efforts were concentrated on strengthening the love of God in all who stepped into the little church, and his unremitting efforts were bent toward giving faith to those who had none, or who had unrewarding beliefs.

The drama of conversion is never easy. Many an individual suffered a painful unwillingness to abandon a path familiar for many years, even if wrong. To these, it seemed frightening to start out along a new tangent. The drama was time consuming. No easy conversion would be as well founded as a conversion made after a profound struggle. The process required above all a firm spiritual leadership, and it required love.

To a man who said that he was reading many books, Padre Pio said, "In books we look for God, in prayer we *find* God."

To save a soul, Padre Pio's patience was long.

A militant materialist, Ferruccio Caponetti, wrote: "In Padre Pio I found a Master. He received me and heard my difficulties and my doubts. Then, in the simplest words, he demolished one by one all my objections, and one by one eliminated all my arguments, thus putting my soul under a naked light. By teaching me the teachings of Jesus, he opened the eyes of my soul to the point where I could see light, and at the same time with his tender words he touched my heart, and I began to believe."

To Alberto Del Fante, a former Mason, who in January 1937 was converted by Padre Pio, the priest said, "You belong to a society which recognizes God but does not love His ministers." In another comment on the Masonic institution, Padre Pio said, "All human conceptions have good and bad, no matter the origin of the conception. One must have the ability to assimilate, to take all the good and offer it to God, eliminating the bad at the same time."

Federico Abresch had first met Padre Pio in 1929. He was a converted Protestant who, as he stated, "had to try again," because his new faith was only lukewarm. "I was brought up in an anti-Catholic family, filled with prejudices against dogmas. I was curious about secret and mysterious things, and one day I found a friend who introduced me to the mysteries of spiritism. Soon I was tired of those inconclusive messages from the beyond, and I passed into the fields of occultism, magical things of all colors and shapes. Then I turned to theosophy, and I was able to manage words like reincarnation, Logos, Brahma, Maja, all the while observing that I was merely enduring through all these sleights-of-hand as I waited for something new and great. When I heard about Padre Pio, described to me as a living Crucifix, continuously making miracles, my curiosity, and also skepticism, made me want to see with my own eyes."

Federico hoped to be rewarded at once for the hardships of his long trip to the monastery. When a reward was not forthcoming at his first meeting with Padre Pio, he felt that the visit had been cold. When he knelt for confession, he gave Padre Pio to understand that, during previous confessions, he had kept quiet about serious sins. Padre Pio then asked if he was in good faith. Federico answered that he believed confession to be a good social institution but that he did not believe in the Divinity of the Holy Sacraments.

"Heresies," said Padre Pio. "Therefore all your Communions have been sacrilegious. It is necessary for you to do a general confession. Examine your conscience and remember when you last confessed well. Jesus has been more merciful toward you than toward Judas." Then, gazing severely over Federico's head, he said, "Praised be Jesus and Mary," and he went on to confess other penitents.

Federico endured agonies, trying to remember when he had last confessed well.

When he returned Padre Pio asked, "So then, when was it the last time?"

Federico began, "Padre Pio, I was a Protestant. . . ."

But Padre Pio interrupted him and said, "All right, so you confessed well the last time when you came back from your honeymoon, so let us start from here."

How did Padre Pio know? How did he know he was married? But Federico did not have time to marvel, because Padre Pio was already enumerating all his sins, even counting out all the obligatory Masses Federico had missed. After the enumeration of the mortal sins, Padre Pio said, "You have been singing a hymn to Satan, when Jesus in His great love has broken His neck for you." He gave Federico his penance and then the absolution.

Such was the impression on Federico that he became a Tertiary of the Order, settling down in San Giovanni Rotondo, where he opened a bookstore.

Pastoral duties made heavy demands on Padre Pio. Yet, to the faithful of his flock, he never seemed hurried, never out of patience. The people who came to him learned, too, that he did not make distinctions between rich and poor, or between social classes. All were souls in his eyes, and given his perception, naked souls at that. Often it would happen that those who insisted on being first, on the grounds that their rank deserved such recognition, would find themselves last. "It is the turn of Benvenuto," Padre Pio would say, and Benvenuto, the chimneysweep of San Giovanni Rotondo, would step ahead of members of European royalty.

Over and above the ordinary work of the priest, Padre Pio had to find time for the many invalids and cripples who came to him, seeking cures. There was much talk of the remarkable efficacy of his prayer, and those for whom doctors saw no hope flocked to him. As they did so, more and more stories were told of his strange powers.

Mrs. Amelia Abresch told of how, a year after her marriage, she had suffered a hemorrhage of the uterus. She consulted Dr. Barbasetti Casanova, and he told her the hemorrhage was caused by a tumor. To verify his opinion, the doctor consulted a specialist, a Professor Monari, and the diagnosis was confirmed. Mrs. Abresch was overjoyed when, not long afterward, she found that she was pregnant. But in July 1926 she had a miscarriage. According to the doctor she then consulted, Professor Orsini Attilio, the miscarriage had been caused by the tumor, which would certainly render natural birth impossible. In case of a second pregnancy, he said, she would have to have a caesarean section. The doctor suggested an operation that would relieve the symptoms of the tumor, but if she had the operation she could not have any children. She refused. In 1929, Professor Silvio Tassinari told her that the tumor had grown so large that surgery was absolutely necessary. "I spoke about my condition to Padre Pio," stated Mrs. Abresch. " 'Padre Pio, the doctors say I must have an operation. What do you advise me to do?' And he answered, 'Follow the advice of the doctors.' To which I said, 'Padre Pio, in that case, I will never have children.' When I told him that, he lifted his eyes to the sky. Very slowly he said, 'Well, my daughter, do not have the operation.' On August 7, 1930, I gave birth to a baby boy."

Countess Baiocchi of Gavinana, residing in Rome, had been sick for a number of years. Various medical tests had failed to reveal the nature of her illness. One day in 1925, when she was taking a walk in Rome, she heard a voice right behind her repeating: "Go to Dr. Festa."

She was sure that the voice pronounced the name of Dr. Festa clearly. Later the same day, she asked her husband if there were in Rome a doctor by that name, and her husband answered that Dr. Festa was one of the doctors who often went to San Giovanni Rotondo to visit Padre Pio, the stigmated priest.

Dr. Festa was in fact the doctor who had operated on Padre Pio himself. When the countess went to him, he had just returned from San Giovanni Rotondo, after performing the operation on the stigmated priest. He, like the other doctors who had examined the countess, was unable to diagnose her illness.

"Countess, are you a religious woman?" asked Dr. Festa. When she answered in the affirmative, he told her about Padre Pio. He explained that Padre Pio was under restriction, and suggested that, since she could not go to see him, she should write a letter.

The reaction of the Baiocchi family was sheer astonishment. They had expected Dr. Festa, like any other doctor, to suggest further consultation with specialists, further tests, and the like. They had never imagined that a doctor would recommend a priest. For the time, the countess did nothing about Dr. Festa's suggestion. However, early in 1930, the countess' illness came to a frightening crisis. Her husband then remembered Dr. Festa's advice and went to San Giovanni Rotondo. He was sick at heart when he spoke with Padre Pio.

He plainly said: "Padre Pio, my wife is dying."

"Pray."

"Pray? But, Padre Pio, she is dying. It is an immediate thing."

"Your despair does not help matters. Try to be calm."

"Padre Pio, why did I come here?"

"Who called you? Pray and hope. Go now, be calm. The Lord is merciful."

"Will you pray for her?"

"Of course."

"With so many people here, asking you to pray for them, will you remember my wife's name?"

"Some names return into my prayers constantly, others do not."

"My wife is in great danger."

"Tell her I am praying for her."

When the count arrived in Rome and told his wife Padre Pio was praying for her, the countess asked to be taken to him. She stayed in San Giovanni Rotondo for two weeks. Before she left, a few days after Easter in 1930, she told Padre Pio that she was cured.

Giuseppina Marchetti, of Bologna, told her story in a newspaper interview in September 1932. Some years earlier, she had suffered a serious fracture of her right arm. She was operated on in Bologna, and the right shoulder bone was extracted. At the time, the doctors hoped that the missing piece of bone might be replaced by new bone growth, but after three years had passed without this development, the doctor who had performed the operation told her that too much time had passed. Since the bone growth had not occurred by then, it would not. Her right arm would remain permanently paralyzed.

The Marchetti family took the girl, then fourteen years old, to San Giovanni Rotondo, where Padre Pio received them "with fatherly love" and comforted them with the following words: "Do not despair. Have faith. The arm will be cured." The Marchetti family returned to Bologna. "Padre Pio had said that I should free myself of the cast and the medical apparatus on September 17, 1932. I had worn the apparatus for three years. I took it off on September 17 and my arm was well."

Grazia Siena was born blind. At twenty-nine, she was still blind. She would often go to the convent and kneel at Padre Pio's feet begging to see the light of day. Padre Pio would often put his hands on her head. One day, he told her she should have an operation on her eyes. Her family took her to a number of doctors in search of one who would perform the operation, but all refused. No operation, they insisted, would give her sight. But from the day Padre Pio said: "Have an operation," Grazia Siena was determined to find a doctor who would carry out his order. Finally, in the company of Rosina Pagliara of Foggia, a woman belonging to the parish of St. Thomas, Grazia Siena went to Bari, to the clinic of Professor Francesco Durante. Dr. Durante examined Grazia Siena's eyes and told her he thought a positive outcome unlikely. But, faced with her pleading, and her faith that the operation would give her sight, he at last agreed to try. "But only a miracle can give you sight," he said.

On April 23, 1933, the daily newspaper *Il Resto del Carlino* carried a story about the case, concluding, "When the bandages were removed, Grazia Siena could see. The first face she saw was the face of Professor Durante. The clinic was immediately crowded with people wanting to see Grazia Siena, who had received such grace. She is still in the clinic. When she is able to leave, she plans to return to her native town of San Giovanni Rotondo to see her parents for the first time. Then she will go to thank Padre Pio, who indicated the right way to her and gave her the faith she needed."

Except for the new houses near the monastery, the infirmary, and the two good roads, San Giovanni Rotondo had changed little over the years.

In 1939, another innovation was brought to the area near the Monastery. A few days before Christmas, a group of citizens of Bologna offered Padre Pio a *Via Crucis*. There were sixteen pieces in all, the fourteen stations representing the scenes of the Passion, a statue of the Madonna of the Graces, and a Cross. The sculpture, done in gray marble in bas relief, was the work of Montanari di Pietrasanta. The promoter of the gift was Carolina Giovannini, of Bologna. The blessing of the pieces was performed by the archbishop of Manfredonia, Andrea Cesarano. The Stations of the Cross were placed along the road from the town to the monastery. As Dr. Goffredo Barbacci reported in the newspaper, *Il Resto del Carlino*, "The crowd expressed the greatest joy when

Padre Pio stepped out of the monastery and walked with the people, with whom he stayed for about two hours, outside the monastery."

The people rapidly accustomed themselves to the statues, falling into the habit of making the Stations regularly on their way to the monastery. But for the rest, the town remained unchanged. Heavy rains still flooded the San Giovanni Rotondo streets. When it snowed, even the mail bus stopped, and the only people who moved in the streets were a few black-clad, shawled, silent women. Ever since 1918, they had met at the piazza in town every evening, a little before Vespers, and started out up the road. Spring, summer, or winter, it made no difference. Every evening they met at the piazza and walked in pairs to Saint Mary of the Graces. After twenty-one years, they were still faultlessly punctual, entering the church a few minutes before Vespers. No blizzard, no crisis of any kind except death had stopped or could stop these four, five black-clad women wrapped in a steady silence, veterans of faith. When there was snow, they brought a shovel along to clear a path. When the *bora* blew, up from the Adriatic Sea, they walked up backwards.

Before their eyes, the drama of Padre Pio's life had unfolded. They had known him as the thirty-year-old sick with tuberculosis and pale from long fasting, and as the thirty-one-year-old stigmated priest. They had watched the visits of the Provincial Father and other high personalities of the order, had seen the arrival of the doctors, and their departure, and had witnessed the coming of priests, archpriests, bishops, archbishops, cardinals. Twenty-one Christmases, twenty-one Easters, all the days in twenty-one years, they had counted on their beads.

While at the time of Padre Pio's first, invisible stigmata, Maria Giuseppe had been able to ask specifically, "Padre Pio, what is the matter with your hands?" what could be asked presently could hardly be put into words. And while in his early days in Pietrelcina his mother and the archpriest had been able to follow him, talking with him of his monastic ambitions while they walked Pietrelcina's hills, now, after more than half a lifetime dedicated to God's mercy and God's love, to fasting and penitences and prayers and much suffering in perfect silence, the four, five women saw his zone of piety as boundless, a zone to be understood only through faith. And so, speechless, they only watched him intently, and then spontaneously said: "This is a saint."

The San Giovanni Rotondo postman, a blind man, was another whose faith was great, so great it matched the faith of the women. He had been blind for many years, following a sickness in his youth. One day, early in 1940, he said to Padre Pio, "Well, maybe I should have my sight back. What do you think?" Then he added, "After all, how ugly can the world be. Should I see it?"

"Tell me which you would rather have, the light of your eyes, or the light of the spirit?" asked Padre Pio.

"Oh, I do not know. Let me see," said the postman, pausing and turning his face around vaguely, as blind people do. Then he decided, "Well, I think I'd rather have the light of the spirit."

No more was said and he remained blind.

He was not at all a man of poor faith, for he had spoken without the shadow of a doubt that, firmly believing that if he had chosen to see, Padre Pio would have given him his sight back at once. And the people of poor faith gathered around the postman to ask, "You mean to tell me you had a choice?"

"He told me to choose."

"Just like that? As incredibly as all that?"

"Just so. Padre Pio told me to pick and I picked the inward light because it is better, better for me anyway."

"Well, it is incredible. But in times of troubles, like these times, maybe you did well to pick the light of the spirit, although it is unbelievable. But maybe you are better off not seeing the world as it is today. Yes, Padre Pio is not a man like you and me. What I mean is, once in many centuries there is a man born who is not like you and me. He is very different."

"Certainly Padre Pio is different. He is a saint."

"Ah, but there is where you and I are different, too. We do not see in the same way. You savor your food, you have a family, you can even learn how to read, and in all this we are alike. But if I speak to you of the green trees, and how they turn yellow and then turn red, then we are different. And especially when I speak of all the colors of the sky, you and I are different, for there is no other way to meet the sky but with your eyes. I, in short, have the sky. And you are without the sky. I can describe the sky to you all I want, but at the end, all descriptions will always be incredible matters to you. In the same way, you can tell me all you want that Padre Pio is a saint, has the power of bilocation, makes instantaneous cures of the sick, straightens the crippled, and has the stigmata, and

when you have told me, I still stand in respect to these matters like you in respect to the sky. The sky is not there for the
blind. It is not there for you. But that does not mean it is not
there. It simply means you cannot see it. However, you would
do well to believe, because as a matter of fact the colors are
there and there is the sky. It is the truth."

"I believe in your sky," said the postman. "Now, you believe
that Padre Pio is a saint."

"Wait. The sky is the truth for all those who have eyes, it is
the truth for me. But what about you?"

"For me it is simple. A truth is a truth," said the blind postman. "It is a truth for you and it is a truth for me. Let us go
now into Saint Mary of the Graces. You might learn how to
see Padre Pio so as to believe and in that case you will have
gained a truth."

"It is all very strange. But I come, I come with you."

"You first," said the postman. "You lead, since you say you
have eyes that see."

The postman, like the four, five women, was happy with the
privilege of watching, storing nourishment for his spirit. The
postman and the women blessed the day they were born in
San Giovanni Rotondo, because the monastery was nearby.
That was all. It was enough for them.

Chapter 10

THE PAST YEARS it was as if Italy had been drawn into a spiderweb. Now the spider had struck. Italy's nonbelligerent partnership with Germany changed to active alliance. As the Italian army and Navy joined the victorious Germans, war was extended to the Mediterrean and Africa.

Overnight people found they had nowhere to turn but to the mercy of God, and they came to San Giovanni Rotondo. Padre Pio prayed long for the living who were in the path of death and did not know where to run.

Would bombs drop on San Giovanni Rotondo? Padre Pio would step out of the convent and assure the people who came to him with fear in their hearts. "Go back to your homes. Not one bomb will fall on San Giovanni Rotondo."

Not one bomb? Why not? There was an airstrip nearby. And those who had no faith went on to say, "Why not? After all, it will never be declared an open city."

Day after day, black-clad women in shawls, with rosary and prayer book, serene as ever, entered the church at Vesper time. Below on the plains poured the Nazi columns like a visit from Friday the thirteenth and the croak of the crow.

Short machinegun blasts sounded in the trembling light of

twilight, for not all Italians were resigned to the partnership with the Germans who now infested Italy. Next morning women in black garments and shawls helped bury the bodies, the foreigners of the armored divisions, and the unresigned Italians.

Already there was no bread. There had always been poor people in San Giovanni Rotondo, but now amongst the poor were the rich also. They stood together in one line, those who had never had much to eat and those who had never seen an empty table, and who, until yesterday, could have afforded to be charitable. And there had always been suffering in San Giovanni Rotondo, but now day by day came people with terror on their faces, their breath smelling of hunger. Did the monks have anything to eat? Padre Pio had his own dinner to give.

They were welcome, men without homes, people running away from what until yesterday they had called home. They were welcome to share Padre Pio's plate of vegetables, to kneel on the floor of the little church, and tomorrow, in the half light of the new day, welcome to hear the Mass.

Not far away machineguns sounded. Just who had died now? How many had died during the Mass? Laden with suffering, imploring, Padre Pio held his dialogue with Jesus until full daylight, beseeching His mercy on a land where people now lived in caves, clutching a piece of hard bread dipped in polluted water, their bodies covered with nothing but rags.

On the roads, frantic refugees fell exhausted. Later their bodies would be found, still gripping a stone parapet. Military columns waved, not knowing that a man sitting perfectly still at a crossroad was a corpse.

What Padre Pio saw now was a land of sentryposts, scouting patrols against sniping farmers. Antifascists who shot at Hitler's troops would come to the convent and ask to be hidden, but the monks could not take them in for fear of retaliation. They were forced to consider the possibility of complete destruction in lightning fashion, overnight. The Germans would have no mercy.

And so, while able-bodied men were gone to France, Greece, Africa, the Balkan countries, their wives and children and mothers and fathers hid in caves and prayed.

German military columns poured onto the plains, and quickly climbed the mountains to turn their guns on the shores. Along the way, the Germans trapped Antifascists, and shot them down on the way to prison.

Electric lights went out along the whole coast, from Sorrento down, and the local population, without bread for several days, was trapped in darkness.

One quiet evening late in May of 1943, Orazio sat in the little clearing in front of the monastery. It was a cool, clear evening, and the sharp, angular lines of the convent building seemed softened by the gently fading light. The old man watched the crowd of people still waiting for Padre Pio to hear their confessions. Then he saw a young man walk into the clearing and stop, as if dismayed at the sight of the crowd. The young man, who wore the uniform of the Italian navy, seemed unlike most of the visitors. He did not rush up to the first monk he saw demanding to see Padre Pio, nor did he approach the church. He stood, looking hesitant and a trifle ill at ease. Orazio was attracted by his diffidence, and decided to walk over and greet the young sailor, but before he stood up, he saw Brother Gaudenzio, perhaps acting on the same impulse, approach the boy. Orazio watched the two converse for a moment, and then Brother Gaudenzio turned and led the young man toward the bench under the elm, where Orazio was sitting. Orazio moved to one side, to make room. Brother Gaudenzio said, "Orazio, here is a young man in the navy, come to see Padre Pio. As he must return to duty to-morrow, he will have to wait until after the confessions. A pity they are so late this evening, eh?"

Orazio nodded, and said to the young man pleasantly, "Well, if you must wait, sit down here, where you will be comfortable."

"Thank you," said the sailor. "I do not wish to trouble anyone," he added, "so if I am disturbing you...."

"No, no," Orazio said warmly.

"Good then. I shall sit with you."

Brother Gaudenzio stood by, smiling kindly on the young man.

"You have met Padre Pio before?" Orazio asked.

"No, but I have heard much about him."

"And perhaps you have some problem to put before him?" Brother Gaudenzio suggested.

"No," said the sailor. "I only want to see him. What I have heard is so remarkable that I had to see him with my own eyes. I do not even want to talk with him."

"Ah," said Orazio, and they fell silent. Orazio did not wish to pry, yet it gladdened his heart to hear people talk of his son. "Do you mind," he said, after a moment, "is it rude of me if I ask from whom you have heard of Padre Pio?"

"Not in the least," said the sailor. "I have been with Don Vittorio Felisati, a chaplain in the navy, and he has talked to me of Padre Pio."

"I do not think I know Don Felisati," Orazio said. He was a little disappointed.

"Nor I," said Brother Gaudenzio, "but then, so many people come here, it is difficult to remember them all."

"Don Vittorio himself knows of Padre Pio only indirectly," the sailor explained. "A friend of his, a doctor in Ferrara, told him long ago, in 1934, about a remarkable experience he had had with Padre Pio. When the doctor's son was eight years old, he was stricken with infantile paralysis. The doctor called in specialists in that disease, but they held no hope for the boy. They gave him two months to live, that was all. His mother brought him here to Padre Pio, and Padre Pio blessed the sick boy and said, 'This is the last stage of the sickness.' Now the boy is a medical student. His father, the doctor, told Don Vittorio the story. When the civil war broke out in Spain, Don Vittorio decided to go there with the Red Cross, to take the consolations of religion to the wounded and dying. Before he left, his doctor friend gave him a Crucifix that had been blessed by Padre Pio. Don Vittorio has kept the Crucifix with him ever since, and he attributes many remarkable events he has seen to Padre Pio's intercession."

While the young man was talking, Brother Nicola had

joined Brother Gaudenzio, and the two monks, like Orazio, had listened intently to the sailor's story. When he broke off, Brother Nicola asked, "What sort of remarkable events?"

"Well," said the sailor, "in Spain, Don Vittorio's work with the Red Cross took him to a large hospital. There were fifteen hundred beds, and almost all the patients were victims of wounds received in the fighting. Don Vittorio invoked Padre Pio, saying, 'Padre Pio, you help me. If you are really a saint, you just have to listen to me and help me. Look at this hospital. Look at this slaughter. I put my sick and my wounded under your protection. You think of them. You do it.' And right away the priest was answered. A wounded man called for Don Vittorio, and when the chaplain went to his bedside, he said, 'Padre, I am from Foggia.' The priest said, 'You are saved. Padre Pio is praying for you, and you will soon return to your home.' But the wounded man shook his head and said, 'No, I am dying, but I have had a dream that my brother came home crippled from Ethiopia, and that Padre Pio let him walk again without crutches.' Don Vittorio blessed him with the Crucifix that had been blessed by Padre Pio. After twenty-one days, the wounded man rose and was ready to make the journey back to Italy. On another occasion, two men with deep head-wounds were brought to the hospital in coma. Don Vittorio prayed to Padre Pio for help and blessed them both with the Crucifix Padre Pio had blessed. These two were soon able to walk out of the hospital. Another of the patients was an officer whose spine had been broken. His doctors said he had only a few hours to live. but Padre Pio helped once more when Don Vittorio prayed to him. In that hospital, where there were

37,000 wounded soldiers and civilians, only fifty-five men died.

"When this war broke out, Don Vittorio went into the navy as a chaplain. He was assigned to the hospital ship, *Citta di Trapani*, a ship of only three tons—so small that just one hit would finish it. It was then that I met Don Vittorio, for I sailed aboard the *Citta di Trapani* as a crew member. On his first voyage in the ship, which was sailing to and from Africa, Don Vittorio prayed to Padre Pio to protect his wounded. Between Derna and Tobruk, a plane dropped five bombs on the ship, but although the plane was directly overhead, not one of them hit.

"Then on December 1, 1942, at nine-twenty in the morning, ten miles from Biserte, we were torpedoed. The ship sank in nine minutes, but only nine wounded soldiers died, out of the hundred and twenty wounded in the ship's berths. I myself was not injured, but Don Vittorio was in the explosion itself, and was wounded in the head and in the legs. He could have been lost. Instead, he was able to crawl out of the debris. I was already in the lifeboat when I saw him on the deck, and I called, '*Cappellano*, jump into the sea! Jump! Jump! The ship is sinking!' But he did not really know what he was doing, and he kept picking through the debris on the deck, as if he were hunting for something. I kept shouting to him, but he did not seem to hear me. Just as the ship broke in half, he finally jumped into the sea near the lifeboat, and we were able to drag him aboard. Not until three hours later, when we were on a submarine which had come to our help, did Don Vittorio know what had happened. I saw how he was holding onto that

Crucifix blessed by Padre Pio. If this is not a miracle, what is a miracle?"

Brother Nicola, Brother Gaudenzio, and Orazio kept silent. The young man continued. "In January of this year, Don Vittorio was assigned to the hospital ship *Principessa Giovanni.* I was not with him on the new ship, but he told me later of his experiences aboard her. All went well until April, but then, on the twentieth, as wounded were going aboard in the harbor of Tunisia, the ship was bombed and machinegunned. Don Vittorio clutched the Crucifix and prayed, and not one hit was scored. On May 5, when the ship was carrying eight hundred wounded and sick men, and seventy women and children of Tunisia, it was machinegunned and bombed twice. The first time was at two o'clock, the second time at six o'clock in the evening. Forty bombs were dropped, Don Vittorio told me, twenty each time. The bombs started a fire that lasted for twelve hours. One bomb fell just where Don Vittorio stood, but when it exploded, Don Vittorio found himself standing at the other side of the ship, holding the Crucifix blessed by Padre Pio. How did he get there? Don Vittorio does not know. The bomb did not touch him and he was able to give the last rites to fifty-five dying. The wounded numbered a hundred and six. For thirty hours the ship leaned dangerously. It might sink at any minute. But again, Don Vittorio prayed to Padre Pio, and again Padre Pio helped. The ship was able to make its way very slowly from the rocks of the Zembra Island until it finally reached Trapani. It even managed to continue sailing to Naples. Don Vittorio told me of this just a few days ago. He says Padre Pio helped him all the time.

"Don Vittorio has two young nephews who are also in the war. One is at Cattaro, the other in Greece. Naturally, he worries about them, but he has been praying to Padre Pio for them, too, and nothing has happened to them. Some while ago, Don Vittorio had word that the one in Greece had been shot by the Germans. As you must know, for a time in Greece, the Nazis were shooting Italian officers. But a Capuchin Chaplain who met Don Vittorio in Taranto was able to reassure him, for the Capuchin had access to records pertaining to Italian officers in Greece, and he had not found the nephew in the list of the missing. When Don Vittorio met him, the Capuchin was on his way to San Giovanni Rotondo, so Don Vittorio gave him a letter to Padre Pio. When the monk returned to Taranto he gave Don Vittorio this message from Padre Pio. 'Tell Don Felisati to rest assured for his nephew in Greece because he is alive and is well and eats bread, and let us pray God that He saves him in the same way until the end.' "

By the time the young man had finished his story, it was fully dark, and the line of people waiting for Padre Pio to hear their confessions had dwindled to a few. Brother Gaudenzio suggested to the sailor that he wait inside the church for Padre Pio to leave the confessional, when perhaps the young man might exchange a few words with him. The boy agreed eagerly, and bidding Orazio good evening, he went with Brother Gaudenzio and Brother Nicola into Saint Mary of the Graces. He did not know that the little old peasant he was leaving on the bench under the elm tree was the father of the man he had come to see, and Orazio felt no need to tell him.

He had heard the reverence in the boy's voice, and seen the faith in his eyes. It was enough.

The night of July 10, 1943, Sicily was invaded. A huge armada of 3266 vessels landed under cover of naval artillery, and secured beachheads at Licata, Gela, and Scoglitti. The war took a new turn, and so did the fortunes of San Giovanni Rotondo.

Sicily was conquered in thirty-eight days, and when Sicily fell, Italy lay open to invasion. As bombers from Sicily began to hit Italian ports and communications, people in the North of Italy threatened rebellion. On July 19, 1943, Mussolini asked Hitler for protection. Hitler persuaded the Italian dictator to defend only the North of Italy, but when Mussolini presented Hitler's plan to the Fascist Grand Council of Italy, the plan was voted down by nineteen of the twenty-five councilors. Mussolini was deprived of leadership, and King Victor Emmanuel called Marshal Badoglio to take over.

The German General staff prepared to fight. New Nazi troops reinforced those units already in Italy, and Germany took over the country.

Like a house of cards, the political structure of the third Italy crashed and scattered.

The South, that had suffered so long under so many injustices, had a new burden to bear when it was occupied by the Nazis. The clearing of Saint Mary of the Graces was small, and could not contain all those stranded in the path of warfare as Hitler's troops poured in with the step of final doom. The people vanished in terror as the Nazi settled on the Gargano Mountain. Around the monastery, all was in darkness.

But the darkness would not last for long. Soon after Hitler's troops arrived, every night was light as day as ten square miles of flares illuminated the sky and mountain. Saturation raids cut to pieces the airfields of Foggia and the airstrip near San Giovanni Rotondo. Such raids broke the Nazis counterattacks and forced them to withdraw farther north. They moved away from the British Eighth Army advancing up the Calabrian coast, into the fire of the American Fifth Army around Salerno on September 10, 1943. On September 12, they encountered the fire of the British Tenth Corps around Battipaglia. Finally the American Sixth Corps attacked them south of the Sele River.

The Nazis withdrew, shooting civilian snipers, demolishing ports, town, and villages, destroying the water supply, mining buildings, removing everything that could be carried on wheels. As units left, other units, withdrawing from positions farther to the South, arrived. They too destroyed everything in their path. The Nazis shot the guilty and innocent alike, until a few orphans became a multitude, and a handful of widows grew into a population of women mourning their dead. Those who were able fled before the tide of destruction, and the plight of the refugees became as pitiful as that of those left behind. When the Nazis had stolen all that there was to steal and destroyed the homes of the peasants, they set fire to the land itself.

The people of San Giovanni Rotondo ran to the monastery walls. Once again Padre Pio came out, stood at the door, and spoke to them—this time of Hitler. "The madman will die," he said.

Planes made their daily raids, but not one bomb was dropped on San Giovanni Rotondo.

When the British army captured the great airfields of Foggia and moved north to Termoli on the Adriatic coast, the land was a battlefield, not a country. The American Eighth Army shifted its main drive to the interior along the Appennine Mountains.

Empty towns changed hands several times. One muddy river was crossed and recrossed time and again, one hill captured and recaptured. The people, in the October cold, burned baby cribs and matrimonial beds for lack of firewood, and lone children hid in bushes by the roadside.

Hitler's army left nothing but unburied corpses on the ground. They planned to do the same all the way up to Rome, and from Rome to Berlin—such were the retreating orders of the man Padre Pio had called a madman. The Nazis seized the boys and young men of the cities and towns of Italy, and sent them off by the thousands, to the North, to work camps in Germany, and to Russia.

Many Italians who had fought with the Germans now took off their uniforms and joined the ranks of partisans and guerilla fighters who were helping the Allied armies to push Nazi troops upcountry. Presently there was news of attacks against Fascist headquarters in central and northern Italy. In the people was born a feeling of liberation from evil. Side by side with sorrow about the fate of that part of the country, above the Volturno line, that was still in Nazi hands, there was also a feeling of hope. In the South, at least, Fascism seemed a tragedy of the past.

Antifascists, once they were freed from imprisonment, were filtering through the German lines up North, and as they returned to the South, they brought news of the bombing of Naples. The bombing had destroyed the church of St. Chiara. The museum of the Angevins and the church, burned out, had fallen in ruins. Before the end of September, Naples had become a maimed city. Its power station was so badly damaged that light went out all along the coast. Main water pipes were blown out, and the city was thereafter without drinking water. From the hills the Nazis were firing long range guns, and below Naples no house could be seen still standing. The English bombed Torre Annunziata, a good-sized town south of Naples.

Before the end of September, the Nazis soaked the castle of St. Paul Belsito in gasoline and burned it down, with all its ancient Aragon chancellory papers, parchments, registers, the Farnese papers, the whole history of the Kingdom of Naples. Hitler, it seemed, was not content to destroy just the industrial and economic life of the capital of the southern regions, but must destroy its history and art as well.

From the American army came news of large supplies that had been prepared for Naples, which was now starving. The food would be landed a few days after the Allied occupation of Naples. The Allies also sent word to Naples that all who could prevent the destruction of the port of Naples would be recognized as patriots.

On October 19, 1943, the whole coast of the Southwest was in complete darkness again. Now it was the Nazis whose air-raids terrorized the people, but they were met with fire from American anti-aircraft guns. Inland in the South, all around San Giovanni Rotondo, villages were burned to the ground. Farther up, towns and villages in the region of Abruzzi were wiped out as the Nazis entrenched themselves below Rome toward the east. At last, General Clark had landed in Naples. On October 25, 1943, he reopened the University of Naples with a noble speech.

The liberation of Naples was greeted with joy throughout the South. But in the country, around San Giovanni Rotondo, the situation remained desperate.

There had been no drinking water for three months. There had been no electric light. The bread supply was low. Suddenly it seemed that if the situation continued, there would soon be no wine for the Mass.

People crossing the German lines reached San Giovanni Rotondo on their way farther south and told of massacres of whole populations in the region of Abruzzi. Hitler's troops wiped out villages with point blank cannon shots. The Abruzzi region was next door, and the news of the massacres left the people of San Giovanni Rotondo frozen with terror and compassion. Darkness and silence and suffering oppressed them, and they sank down into the dregs of hopelessness in what seemed like an eternal night stitched patch by patch into endless mourning. At the news that American soldiers were making their way up from Foggia, the suffering people lashed at the mourning sheet that wrapped them, and stepped out of the eighteenth and nineteenth centuries to meet them in the world of today.

Jeeps and trucks arrived, and soldiers jumped out and began to unload food in the shamble of twisted trees and collapsed farmhouses. Not one bomb had fallen on San Giovanni Rotondo, but the guns of retreating Germans, with their scorched earth faith, had wrought desolation enough.

With the gait of appalling suffering, the people of San Giovanni Rotondo, hugging walls, crouching on bent knees, moved away from their dark, unhappy houses to meet the first sight of the twentieth century, and their way of living was put in reverse. Suddenly not the few but the many were free. The large landowners who had gained five mountains for each man in twenty years of Fascism stepped out of their houses to find the world changed. It had changed overnight. They stood blinking at the jeeps, the trucks, the food.

Four, five women and a blind postman led the American soldiers to the clearing of Saint Mary of the Graces to see Padre Pio of Pietrelcina, the stigmated priest.

"He said that not a bomb would be dropped on our town and in fact we have not been bombed, while all other towns have been bombed. We had the airstrip, which now has been wiped out. But no bombs fell on San Giovanni Rotondo."

Padre Pio stepped out of the monastery early in the afternoon of February 2, 1944, to meet the soldiers, the troops just up from Foggia and just off the Salerno beachheads, determined to push on to Rome. He found them battle-weary but still in contact with humanity, in contact enough to say, "Padre Pio? I'm Joe." Padre Pio put his hands on the head of the soldier named Joe, and one by one, on the heads of all the other soldiers who knelt before him. On the morning of February 3, the soldiers came again. They knelt in the little church for Mass, watching Padre Pio's contorted face, his eyes blurred with tears, the live suffering on his brow, his uplifted hands with the wounded palms. And the soldiers saw that San Giovanni Rotondo, battered and half starved, had yet one priceless treasure.

More and more soldiers came, and brought more and more supplies.

"Bread? Yes, you have brought bread up, but please, if you can, since the Nazi troops have taken all the wine, if you can bring up a little wine for Padre Pio's Mass. It is about finished the friars say. Can you?"

They brought the white wine, and they unloaded more bread out of huge trucks. San Giovanni Rotondo gathered to watch, lined up for the distribution of the food. But it was not bread alone that had started to change everything, but something else. Orazio, and the others who, like him, had commuted to America and back, recognized this something else.

The army could have arrived, camouflaged and mud-caked, with nothing but their rifles, with no supply trucks, no cigarettes and candy-bars, and the something else would have started the change. It came overnight, and it was a new experience for the people of the South. It was the feel of freedom.

Presently soldiers were looking hurriedly for relatives. But there was little time to seek out families, because the soldiers had to hurry to help with the seven last miles from Cisterna to Rome.

"I think I have heard of the people you are looking for," said the San Giovanni Rotondo folks. "If I meet any of them, what should I say your name is?"

"Salvatore. Sal."

"Very well, I will remember. Do you know what it means?"

"What? My name?"

"Yes. It means Saviour."

As they returned to Foggia and Salerno and Naples and Taranto and Bari and Brindisi, the soldiers said to other soldiers, "There's a monk up there, a priest the folks call a saint, and he's got bleeding hands. I've seen them myself. Be sure you see that monk."

"Be sure you see." That was the beginning. It was followed by, "Be sure you help."

As they rolled to Cisterna to liberate Rome from the clutches of the German General Staff, wave after wave of soldiers paused at the monastery. They were men of many nations—American, British, Canadian, French, Polish, North African, South American. All appeared at the crack of dawn to attend Padre Pio's long Mass, and waited to be confessed by the stigmated priest.

"Hey, he don't understand a word of English, but he understood me all right."

They were visiting Padre Pio all day long, arriving in jeeps and camions and lorries which they parked around the elm tree in the cobbled clearing.

Italy from Rome up remained in Nazi hands throughout February of 1944. In March, the Allies were still seven miles below Rome, and still below the Cassino Benedictine monastery. Suddenly, early in March the news spread in the North of Italy that Padre Pio was dead, had just died. Thousands of people who loved him dearly and were caught in Nazi territory refused to accept what was said for truth, but they had no way to investigate. As the rumors of his death became insistent, the people finally accepted them.

They found out the truth slowly. On March 26, 1944 the Fifth Army began to roll up from the Anzio garrison and the British Eighth Army, with French and Polish units, replaced the Fifth Army around Cassino and pushed up. With forces concentrated on the west and in the center of Italy, pressure was turned toward Rome. Polish troops cut over Cassino. The Fifth Army opened the ancient Appian Way and the Casilina Way, the road to Rome. And on June 4, 1944 the Fifth Army captured the Eternal City.

Since the autumn of 1943, when Mussolini's leadership had been repudiated by King Victor Emmanuel, the Fascist dictator had governed the Nazi occupied North under the protection of the Germans. He had called the country under his authority "the Republic of Salo." Throughout the bitter winter, *Il Duce*'s continued power had been a constant source of terror to all Italians. Despite the advances of the Allies, Mussolini continued to regard himself as the head of the government, and would not give up his role as dictator. Finally, in April of 1945, just over a year after the fall of Rome, the Republic of Salo crumbled. On April 28, the dictator was captured and executed by partisans as he attempted to flee toward Valtellina, over the Alps.

The North of Italy then finally learned the truth that Padre Pio had not died, but was still in San Giovanni Rotondo. In their joy, they joined the thronging pilgrims from the South, and from other lands, and made the long journey to the little monastery at San Giovanni Rotondo. They had to see for themselves that their beloved saint still lived. The crowds jamming the clearing before the monastery became larger than ever. It was a crowd of free people, free to choose, in the aftermath of the bloodiest war yet, to start anew from any given point. They wished to begin this way, with a Mass said by Padre Pio.

Brother Agostino with his bamboo cane hardly hoped to restrain the rush into Saint Mary of the Graces. Just the same he tried, as best he could, often begging the people to act in an orderly fashion at the top of his voice.

When Padre Pio stepped to the altar, Brother Agostino would plead with the pilgrims, "Good people, why have all of you come here? He is a priest like any other. Do you think that his absolution is a double absolution?"

The other eight monks tried to help him, but in the end of April and the first week of May there were over seven thousand people in and out of Saint Mary of the Graces. In the face of such numbers, there was little the friars could do to help.

The people asked Padre Pio to pray for them more now than before: the country was in shambles and the Italians were stunned. And Padre Pio prayed. He thanked the Lord that

Rome and Florence and Pisa and Siena and Bologna and Venice, which could not have been rebuilt, not by Italians or Allies or Russians or anyone else, had not been destroyed as other towns and hamlets, which could be rebuilt, had been destroyed. There were eight hundred miles of mountains and hills and plains and shores on which gas drums had been dumped and drained, so as to burn five thousand years of human labor and ingenuity. Padre Pio prayed fervently for recovery.

To the people of San Giovanni Rotondo, and also to the people of London, to those of Calais, to those of all the other towns that had been tramped asunder, he repeated that God is love and that yesterday's darkness would surely turn into light tomorrow. He gave hope without pause where hope was desperately needed.

San Giovanni Rotondo, like the other towns that had become debris, had to start quickly on the way to recovery. Mourning had to be brief, even if deeply compassionate, for today it was no longer possible to mourn the dead long. If weeping devoured the energy of the people today, then local infections would spread, and grow into a plague.

Below San Giovanni Rotondo the plains were all wreckage, all the way from Foggia to Manfredonia. Now when he rose to pray in the middle of the night, his prayer was that the Lord might give people the strength necessary for the job at hand. A profound silence rose from those plains. But over such a silence sounded the peels of the Saint Mary of the Graces' bell, seemingly tolling far off up the mountain, yet arriving down below with sweet and gentle tones. Other countryside churches, shelled into rubble, were silent. Still others stood filled with the empty cartridges and empty wine bottles and cigarette butts and chow-greased mess-gears and live ammunition left behind by the Nazi army.

Only now, as people could move about freely, the enormity of the damages was fully discovered. People recounted it to Padre Pio, weeping before him without restraint because they knew him to be kind and loving. He responded with prayers. After he had heard a hundred voices and had gathered onto himself all their sorrows and suffering, he went to offer them up to the Crucified Christ. From Vespers on he knelt in solitude. He gave himself no rest whatever, no pause. In a feverish determination to be heard by the Lord, he rested no more than three hours out of twenty-four.

No sooner were the Nazis driven out of Italy when a new menace appeared. In the conclamation of the new era, all voices were to be heard. Otherwise, the people reasoned, democracy would be crippled before it could take hold. But among the voices, in the cities and in the country alike, were inevitably some belonging to Communists. In San Giovanni Rotondo, these voices clamored for a Communist Administration for the region of Puglie.

Politics were none of Padre Pio's business because he was a monk, a priest. But when people asked him how they should cope with the Communists, he answered them. His advice was to be sure to become more Christian.

"If Christians were more Christian there would be no need

for Communism," answered Padre Pio. And he criticized the Catholics with the severity of St. Paul.

When any of the San Giovanni Rotondo Communists entered Saint Mary of the Graces, Padre Pio would ask for their party membership cards.

"Let me have this," he would say. Then he would tear the card up, saying, "You do not need this in Heaven."

"But, Padre Pio, I am not in Heaven. I am here and I am unemployed and I have the promise of a job. Now you tore up my card. . . ."

"You do not need it," repeated Padre Pio. "Neither can you live on promises. Accept work from Saint Francis. Go now and come back ready to work on the road."

Chapter 11

Long before the war, Padre Pio had begun to dream of a realistic, practical way to help the many sick people and cripples who visited San Giovanni Rotondo. He had first mentioned the idea of a hospital close by the monastery in a letter he wrote to two doctors in the town, during the time that he was restricted in the monastery. In 1929, when the restrictions had been lifted, he had longed to begin work on the project, but the funds at his disposal were then far too limited for such an undertaking. Widening roads, yes, that could be done. And a free infirmary in town. But a hospital? Still, Padre Pio had clung to his dream.

In 1939, when the trouble that became the holocaust of World War II was just beginning to gather momentum, Padre Pio had said to the two doctors who were his friends, "If the infirm is Christ, the place where the infirm is cured must be a tabernacle." During the same year, he had had a prophetic conversation with his personal doctor, Guglielmo Sanguinetti of Ravenna. Dr. Sanguinetti was then head of the medical service of the state railway. He had been talking with Padre Pio of his plan to practice in Borgo San Lorenzo when he retired from the railway commission on a pension, and Padre Pio had remarked, "Maybe you will like to live in San Giovanni Rotondo, instead."

And Dr. Sanguinetti had answered, "Well, the pension the state will provide when I retire will not be large, you know. I will need the income from my office in Borgo San Lorenzo. San Giovanni Rotondo has well established doctors of its own. It is a small town, and I will not be needed here."

"We will see," Padre Pio had said. Had he revealed that he was then, despite Italy's increasing poverty, thinking of a large hospital, it would have sounded insane.

"Do you mean I might work at the infirmary?" Dr. Sanguinetti had asked.

"No," Padre Pio had said, "we will see, in due time."

What could be a better time? Padre Pio asked himself in 1945, as he surveyed the ruins of his country. On Christmas in 1945, over five hundred invalids made their way to the convent. Not all had incurable diseases. Medical care could help them. But to provide medical care for five hundred people, that would require a hospital. Besides, it would take a great deal of labor to construct such an institution, and the people who had survived the war needed nothing so much as they needed work.

To start realizing his dream, Padre Pio asked American officials in the government of occupation for help with the initial cost of the project. The Americans had adequate equipment, the heavy machinery that would be needed to cut away the mountain that rose so close to the monastery that its base was but a few yards from the left side of the little church.

Thousands of tons of earth and huge rocks would have to be blasted and removed if building were to be done on the site. The government of occupation promised to let him know if it could find a way to help. But they did not find a way. Instead, they informed him that such an extended project would cost too much, and was therefore impractical.

In twenty-seven years of constant dedication to the needy, Padre Pio had received donations in amounts ranging from a few lire to hundreds and thousands. But this money had already been used. He had given it to houses of the poor, to orphans, and to the small infirmary he supported in town. If a great new hospital were to become a reality, he would have to begin raising funds in earnest. As a first step, he decided to broach the subject to a few intimate friends.

Early in January 1946, Padre Pio gathered a few of these friends and held a meeting in his cell. Among those attending were Dr. Sanguinetti, Dr. Mario Sanvico from Perugia, and Dr. Carlo Kisvarday a pharmacist from Zara, whose house had been destroyed during the war. Padre Pio told them, "I would like to build a large home to give hospitality to the many pilgrims who climb up here and beg for miracles. Faith and hope will make their spirits well, but with charity we would build a roof over the heads of these pilgrims. Then science, if it can, will do the rest." Padre Pio revealed to his friends that the hospital project was a sort of passion for him.

"A big hospital," Dr. Sanguinetti said thoughtfully.

"Not the usual hospital," Padre Pio said. He explained that he did not want to call it a hospital at all. A "House for the Relief of Suffering," that was closer to what he had in mind.

The institution should be a home with a genuine Christian meaning, rather than the usual hospital with its cold mechanics.

The doctors sympathized enthusiastically with the idea, but to them it seemed impossible. The expense of such an undertaking would be staggering, at any time, and in the time of appalling hardship that followed the war, how could it be thought of?

"You must help me," Padre Pio told them. They frankly could not see how they might help, yet they agreed.

"You," said Padre Pio, turning to Dr. Sanguinetti, "will come to live at San Giovanni Rotondo, and you will be of much help."

"Padre Pio," the good doctor answered in confusion, "I know you have long wanted me to settle in San Giovanni Rotondo. I remember that we talked of it even before the war. And I would like nothing better, believe me. But we are none of us rich these days. I have to make a living. I need my practice in Borgo San Lorenzo."

Padre Pio lifted his eyes to the clear sky visible from the cell window, "Well. . . . there is the ticket, I am telling you that you will come to live here."

"Ticket? What ticket?" asked Dr. Sanguinetti. He could only think Padre Pio might mean a railroad ticket, for Dr. Sanguinetti had worked for the state railway for many years, and it was conceivable that they would give him a complimentary ticket.

Padre Pio did not explain.

It pained Dr. Sanguinetti to have to refuse his friend's request, and when he left San Giovanni Rotondo for Borgo San

Lorenzo after the meeting, he was in a sorrowful mood. He could only console himself with the thought that perhaps Padre Pio knew something he did not know. The mysterious ticket, what was that? Dr. Sanguinetti thought about it often, and wondered.

In the spring of 1946, a little before Easter, Dr. Sanguinetti was called to the house of a wealthy nobleman, Giovanni Sacchetti, who was vacationing with his family in Borgo San Lorenzo. Don Giovanni's son had been taken ill. Fortunately, the boy's illness was not serious, and Dr. Sanguinetti had no difficulty in treating it. The grateful parents pressed their hospitality on him, and he was glad of the opportunity to talk with them in friendly circumstances. He lost no time in bringing up the subject of Padre Pio's hospital, tactfully implying that perhaps the wealthy Sacchetti family would like to contribute. He spoke of his confidence in Padre Pio, and described his friend's remarkable powers. In the course of the conversation, he brought up the subject of the ticket Padre Pio had mentioned. "I do not know what sort of ticket. I have been wondering about it ever since January, asking myself, what can this ticket be? But I am sure it will be something." The Sacchettis were politely interested, but made no move to volunteer contributions. As the doctor was leaving, Don Giovanni Sacchetti said to him in what seemed to Sanguinetti a joking manner, "Do be sure to let me know what that ticket is, when you find out." Dr. Sanguinetti felt mortified that his blind faith had seemed amusing to the Sacchettis.

But a few days later, he was back at the nobleman's house, his mortification gone and a triumphant exultation taking its place. "I have indeed found out what that ticket Padre Pio mentioned is. Once I bought a government bond, and now I have received the news that my bond has won a bond number state prize. It is a modest fortune, but a fortune just the same. Now I am free to leave my office and try to help Padre Pio build the hospital."

The attitude of the Sacchetti family changed at once. They needed no other proof to be convinced that Padre Pio could read the future. How was Padre Pio to know, otherwise, that the doctor's bond would win a prize? In the first place, how would Padre Pio know that the doctor had bought a bond? Don Giovanni Sacchetti, no longer laughing, was ready to put his money into the hospital project. Not only that, he would also collect money from his friends.

A legal organization of Padre Pio's friends was set up for the project. Dr. Kisvarday was elected administrator, Dr. Sanvico vice-president, Mr. Sacchetti president. Dr. Sanguinetti would be the head of the clinic when it opened. To manage the construction job, the committee called in a young engineer-architect from the Abruzzi region named Angelo Lupi. But he was very doubtful about his ability to carry on the job. "Padre Pio," he said, "I do not even have a degree. I am a few months short of my architect degree. Would you not prefer to find somebody else?"

"Do not worry about your degree. God will give you your degree."

Mr. Sacchetti had given generously, and Dr. Sanvico, who had inherited a good deal of money from his merchant family in Perugia, had contributed his capital. Dr. Sanguinetti had

turned in most of the small fortune of the state prize, keeping
only what he would need to live. Yet this money was gone by
June of 1946. The base of the mountain was still almost intact,
except for two hundred fifty yards of blasted rock. But the
soldiers of all nations who had visited Padre Pio during the
war had been impressed, and they remembered him. Most of
them had returned to homes that were prosperous compared
to the poverty they had seen in Italy. They wrote to Padre
Pio, and sent donations, so that the work did not stop. Poor
people in San Giovanni Rotondo went to church and prayed
for the happiness of the soldiers who had not forgotten that a
friar way up a desolate mountain had a dream.

Newspapers in Rome carried the news, in the summer of
1946, that Padre Pio had begun to level the side of the Gargano
Mountain next door to Saint Mary of the Graces to build a
large hospital. Laborers were using makeshift tools. The
architect, Angelo Lupi, used an ordinary kitchen table for a
drawing board. He had it set up in one of the rooms of the
monastery.

There was such a lack of machinery, equipment, and materials that Angelo Lupi soon lost all hope, and so did the blind
postman of San Giovanni Rotondo who stood at his side.

Angelo told Padre Pio of his discouragement. "Padre Pio,"
Angelo said, "if the men have to work with this equipment it
will take twenty years to finish the job. I very much doubt
that we can do it at all. The mountain alone will require. . . ."

Padre Pio put his hand in the pocket of his robe, searched
deeply in the pocket, and pulled out a small gold coin—the
coin a Southerner in Italy always keeps. He showed the coin

to Angelo with a smile, as a Southerner does, satisfied with himself for having saved a gold coin over the decades. Then he said, "I want to make the first offer for the right equipment and the material."

It was obvious now to Dr. Sanguinetti and Dr. Sanvico, and to the administrator, Carlo Kisvarday, that somehow the project would materialize out of Padre Pio's determination. Their faith in him was so great that they went to get their families, to settle them permanently in San Giovanni Rotondo. For the time being, prefabricated houses would have to do, although they wondered if they would be safe against the fierce northeast wind.

Work went on. Like Padre Pio's intimate friends, the laborers had faith in the offer of the gold coin, faith that somehow it would be speedily multiplied. And sure enough, one day soon after, the blind postman walked into the convent with a few lire in his hands, looking for Padre Pio. He gave Padre Pio the money and said, "For the House for the Relief of Suffering."

"This is the second offer," answered Padre Pio with a smile.

Right behind the postman stood the four, five women wrapped in their black shawls. They did not even speak when they gave their few lire.

"And this is the third," said Padre Pio.

The fourth offer was quite different, and it brought great hope. An English newspaperwoman named Barbara Ward heard of Padre Pio's project and was fascinated by the idea. She thought the plan to build a hospital on the Gargano a noble and imaginative stroke of inspiration and began to write

of it for her newspaper. Barbara Ward also spoke of the project to Fiorello La Guardia, ex-Mayor of New York City and,
at the time, Director-General of UNRRA. Fiorello La Guardia well knew what the conditions of Southern Italy were, not
only because he had seen them with his own eyes on his various
trips there as Director of UNRRA, but also because his father,
born in a small town near Foggia, had described to him the
squalor of those exploited regions. The project of the hospital
interested Fiorello La Guardia a great deal—so much that he
provided three hundred and forty thousand dollars of unused
UNRRA funds. The hospital committee agreed with the
American government that they would call the hospital the
"Fiorello La Guardia Clinic." No other demand was made on
the generous offer.

The people of San Giovanni Rotondo went to church at
once. On their knees, they prayed, "Oh Lord, bless Fiorello
La Guardia." It was American money, just as solid as the gold
coin of Padre Pio.

Four million people were unemployed in Italy, but suddenly, no one would be unemployed in San Giovanni Rotondo
and nearby towns.

After the referendum of June 1946, when Italy decided for
a republic, the government was planning various programs for
the relief of the South. Municipal Aid Boards were set up,
representing a national expenditure of ten billion lire. The
Ministry of the Interior created the Summer and Winter
Assistance Fund, with an expenditure of twenty-five billion
lire. The Southern Italy Fund, which was established at the
same time, was not a mere assistance plan, but a progressive
project designed to increase productivity in the South by

transforming the structure of the Southern economic system. The Fund would undertake to supply to all communes in the South some thirty-three hundred billion lire. The money would transform the productivity of some three million acres of land and would bring irrigation to some two million eight hundred thousand acres of mountain zones.

Of the total expenditure, 32 per cent would go to land reclamation, irrigation, and transformation; 20 per cent to land improvement; 11 per cent to the construction of aqueducts and sewers, and 9 per cent to roads. The program called for surfacing seven thousand miles of country roads and building anew another thousand miles.

But it was not an easy undertaking for a country that had lost as much as Italy had lost. The region of Venetia Giulia, which had been a part of Italy since World War I, was gone now, and so was all of the African territory. Libya, Eritrea, and Somaliland, which had been colonized before the advent of Fascism, were no longer under Italian rule. The government planned improvements, to be sure, and was hard at work at them, but progress must necessarily be slow.

People in Foggia knew they would have work at once. Communism would be checked. Most important, the sick would finally have their hospital. The section for infantile paralysis in the Fiorello La Guardia Clinic would be the first one in all the South, with its population of a thousand people to each square mile.

Padre Pio sat every day in the confessional, leaning his head to the right and to the left, his hands returning to adjust the confessional doors, his fingers delving from time to time in

the tiny box of cedarwood herbs. The expression on his face
was completely attentive. And the people responded to his
love not only with love. They gave as much as they could. He
sat at ease, comfortable in the confessional box, and the people
felt at east after having made their donations. At times, people
actually gave their last lira, offering it without fear of being
left without money.

And people in San Giovanni Rotondo said, "Yes, it looks as
if the hospital will be built. It is the only way to relieve conditions, because only employment will help us."

Because of bureaucratic difficulties, the three hundred forty
thousand dollars provided by Fiorello La Guardia was delivered by fits and starts, not all at once. The doctors themselves, and the pharmacist from Zara and the architect, Angelo
Lupi, rented, leased, and bought enough machinery and equipment and materials to make the friars blink.

By September 1946, the base of the mountain had been
blasted and enough ground had been leveled for the founda-
tion of the building.

Padre Pio sat in the confessional, close to the front door of
the church, while the blasting made the church floor quiver.

The activity, the white-gray and red dust from the mountain, the sound of the blasting, the laborers singing at their
work pleased Padre Pio, and did not distract him from his
own work in the confessional. On his way in and out of the
church, he would often pause at the front door to watch
Angelo Lupi, the architect, poring over his blueprints, feverish
with work, and happy. There were toolsheds at the construction site, and work space where the materials needed in the

construction could be manufactured on the spot. It was cheaper to work from raw materials than from finished products, and the extra work made room for more employees than would have been needed otherwise.

Padre Pio saw the diligent industry of his people, and was well content. Perhaps all the governments from now on would gear themselves to the ingenuity of the man in the street, speed the common man without crushing him with bureaucracy. Perhaps now governments would allow the people themselves to bridge the gap from the Southern regions to the Northern. The people of the South had curiosity and will enough to go North and work in the industrial plants, in the midst of people who were better fed, better clothed, and better educated. Perhaps, too, industrial plants would come South. Left free to move about as they wished, the people might do so many concrete things to relieve Southern unemployment. All the South wanted was a chance to work. Then, instead of rushing into the Communist meeting rooms, folks would peacefully shuttle from home to work and back home again, and from home to church on Sunday.

Padre Pio's satisfaction at the building was no greater than Orazio's. The genial old man who always had a word for everyone had been delighted with the new project from the outset. When contributions had begun to come from American soldiers, he had been even more delighted. Fiorello La Guardia's help was a source of genuine pride to him. Always, Orazio had enjoyed his role as the man who understood America and its machinery, and he admired America fiercely. How often, during the war, had he suffered at hearing people say to him,

"Look, Ora, what your friends have done." Then he could only sigh resignedly. But with the Americans helping to build the hospital, Orazio could again be proud of "his friends."

The people were fond of Orazio. They called him Ora, and in the long hot summer afternoons would sit with him in the shade of the elm tree. Of late they had been complaining to him about their newest troubles. "We have too many Communists in San Giovanni Rotondo. It is incredible, just where Padre Pio has never stopped proving that there is God."

Every day, in good weather, Orazio sat in the shade of the elm tree minding his five great-grandchildren. These were the sons and daughters of his first son Michele's daughter, married to a San Giovanni Rotondo landowner. Of the children, the second-born and the first son, Alfonso, was Padre Pio's favorite. Alfonso, who was called Fofolino, returned Padre Pio's affection. One winter Fofolino was asked to give his overcoat away. He did not want to part with it. "Uncle, I will be cold. I want to give it to the poor but I will be cold," he had said. Padre Pio had answered, "Well, today you do not get a kiss." And the boy had said, "Wait. I give it. Now what about my kiss?"

These bright days in the summer and autumn of 1946, when Orazio sat looking after the little ones and watching the construction of the new hospital and talking with the people of San Giovanni Rotondo, were the happiest of Orazio's life. They were also the last. One day, late in September, the old man, who was now eighty-six years old, was taken ill. He was put to bed in Mary Pyle's house—not the grand building that housed the Tertiary of the Order, but the little home she had built when she first arrived. It was the house in which Maria Giuseppe had died. Orazio was not destined to see the Fiorello La Guardia Clinic completed. He was not to feel the fierce *bora* again, nor to greet another spring, nor to see his great grandchildren a year older. For two weeks, he lay too ill to rise from his bed. Every day Padre Pio sat by his bedside. At the first sight of suffering and death, long ago in Pietrelcina, the child Francesco had turned his eyes to his *Tata*. Now those same eyes rested upon the same *Tata*, but it was his suffering and his death that they witnessed. On October 7, 1946, with his son at his bedside, Orazio died.

The funeral was attended by the members of the Third Order, since Orazio had been a member himself. The funeral cortege advanced, with the band playing a funeral march behind the coffin, through the beehive of Orazio's beloved construction. Drills and blasting stopped for the funeral, but the red dust was still settling on the road when the coffin was brought out of the church. The procession wound through streets heaped to the sides with fresh earth from a gash in the ground extending for miles to the regional water system, past ovens for baking brick, past furnaces for lime, gravel machinery and stored gravel twenty feet high, past the yard for the production of cement, the yard for artificial marble, the yard for lumber and carpentry, to the cemetery where Maria Giuseppe was buried. It was a large procession, for crowds of relatives and friends attended the funeral. But Padre Pio did not. He could no longer walk that far on his wounded feet. As the mourners passed on the way to the cemetery, it began to snow, just as it had snowed during Maria Giuseppe's funeral.

As the mourners walked bare-headed behind the coffin, farmhouse folk along the way made the sign of the Cross. "It is a fine funeral," they said to one another.

In the sad procession walked a seventeen-year-old girl, a spiritual daughter of Padre Pio's, who believed that he had interceded with the Lord to save her life. During the war, she had been accused of Fascist crimes and had been caught one day by a group of Antifascists. Taking her to a spot in the open fields, they had stood her against a boulder and then moved away from her to assume the traditional position of the firing-squad. But before they could fire, a military column appeared, and the girl ran away. There were many soldiers in the column. For ninety-six hours, the troops were passing through San Giovanni Rotondo. While there were soldiers in and around the town, the Antifascists dared not show themselves. By the time they could leave their homes again, they had discovered that they had caught the wrong girl.

The snow stopped, and when the cortege returned through town and back to the convent, the work of construction was again in full swing.

It was months despite the hard work of the laborers before the actual construction of the clinic could get under way. The ceremony for the laying of the first pink stone took place after Easter in 1947. Italian and American officials attended the ceremony. Among the churchmen was the Provincial Father of the Capuchin Order, Father Paolino di Casacalente. Monsignor Cesarano, Bishop of Manfredonia, sent archpriest Professor Principe as his representative. Some fifty officials of the democratic government were present. The guests were received by Mr. Sacchetti, Dr. Sanvinco, Dr. Kisvarday, and Angelo Lupi.

Padre Pio did not speak at the ceremony, but in private conversations, he told visitors that he hoped the South would no longer be bypassed. To his mind, he said, it had been bypassed since the Kingdom of the Two Sicilies. The South would fall as a burden on the shoulders of the next hundred governments unless now, with the new spirit of renewal, freedom, and democracy, a common ground could be found between the interests of North and Central Italy and the interests of the South. Familiarity and love must unite Italy, and the Southerner must no longer be a second-class citizen.

The Fiorello La Guardia Clinic would have medical care for all, whatever region people came from. It would accept sick people from everywhere in the world, whatever their race. Fees would be the same for the rich as for the poor.

Visitors agreed that the site of the hospital was as beautiful as the Italian Riviera. The clinic would overlook a chain of rugged mountains, and the Manfredonia Sea, visible in the distance, completed the view.

When people asked, "Just how many wards should the clinic have?" Padre Pio replied, "Wards? No wards."

The House for the Relief of Suffering, Padre Pio insisted, must not be too much like a hospital. It would be all right to have four beds in each large, comfortable room, but there must be no wards. The administrator wondered just how many patients Padre Pio wanted in the clinic. Why, all. All the people who needed the Fiorello La Guardia Clinic.

Said Padre Pio, "How would you like to be in sight of Heaven and be told there is no room for one more?"

"But, Padre Pio, as it is it looks as if the hospital will cost millions. Besides, it is a building and any building will contain just so many people and no more."

"Well, the main building can have wings later on. We are leaving room at the sides for such wings, because no one who wishes to come should be turned away. The present plan calls for a large library, too. In case more room is needed, the space of the library can be used."

"Padre Pio, we will end up broke before the roof is put on," said the worried administrator. "I was suggesting that we could use other marble rather than this costly Carrara marble for all the stairways, and the costly red Carso marble."

"The eye must be pleased," answered Padre Pio.

Padre Pio begged the doctors and the administrators to be bold and to have courage. Why caution and fear? Was not this a good cause? Indeed it was, and it would counteract at least some of the sinful lavishness of the world. Why should the scale be so heavy on the side of crime and depredation, and so light on the side of comfort for the sick? When would the man with a little of something left over stop running to those who had already eaten plenty and turn to the needy? Well, things would have to change.

"But, Padre Pio," the administrator protested, "what about the convent? The walls need...."

"San Francesco thinks about the monastery. Put the money into the House for the Relief of Suffering."

The House for the Relief of Suffering would be a start in

boldness that might spark the imagination of the rest of the South, and even inspire the rest of the country to commence great works again.

Soon the men involved in the plan began to understand that they need not fear. When the first million dollars was gone, they found that they had another five hundred thousand dollars. By the time this sum was spent, they found ready still another five hundred thousand. Offers and donations came in from all parts of the world. And soon the men involved began to understand what Padre Pio meant when he said, "The grace of God is enormous, and a single act of love toward God has so much value in His eyes that He would consider small things given as big as the universe. Love is the spark of God in men, the very essence of God personified in the Holy Spirit. We, poor creatures, should dedicate to God all the love of which we are capable, and our love, to be adequate for the Lord, should be infinite. We must remain aware that only God is infinite, but although we can therefore never achieve our goal, let us put all our energy into our love for God. Thus one day He can tell us: 'I was thirsty and you gave me to drink, I was hungry and you gave me food, I was suffering and you comforted me.' The man who, surpassing himself, bends over the wounds of the unfortunate brother, sends up to God the most beautiful of all prayers, one made of sacrifices, of love lived and realized, of dedication in the body and in the spirit. In every man who is sick there is Jesus who suffers, and in every man who is poor there is Jesus who is abandoned, as in every sick man who is poor and sick there are twice Jesus who suffers and is abandoned."

Chapter 12

On the day of the ceremony, when the cornerstone was laid, Angelo Lupi, the architect, had a day of rest. At daylight the following morning, he resumed his work.

After Mass that morning, Padre Pio paused in the doorway of the church and watched Angelo. Dr. Kisvarday, leaving the church, stopped near Padre Pio and remarked, "Angelo is working too hard. He should take a few days rest, not just one day."

"If he needs it he knows he can rest," answered Padre Pio. "But I assure you that he is the sort of man who gains in health as he works, and does not eat bread as well when he rests."

And indeed it did seem that Angelo was thriving on his work. As time wore on, Angelo worked ever harder and harder.

Bareheaded, the collar of his jacket turned up at dawn and again after sundown, he shuttled without pause between workmen and from toolsheds to building. He stood still for a few minutes only at noon, when he ate his lunch of bread and cheese, the food in one hand and his blue prints in the other. He had not gone back to the Abruzzi, to visit his family, since 1946, and although Padre Pio had not asked him, it was obvious that he would not visit his home until he had finished, or, as Padre Pio put it, earned his degree.

At noon, as Angelo paused, he stood with his back turned to the monastery, facing and looking at the mountain, half of which he had excavated, the building, the whole construction ground with its machinery. When he finished his lunch and moved again, Padre Pio would see his face, squinting, pondering on the blueprints. Perhaps what he mused on was not so much the work in progress as the fact of Italy's great architectural heritage. In this country, the message of Jesus Christ spoke from ancient stone edifices, and inimitable works in marble, almost all of them unique, which stood over the centuries as though erected only yesterday. The dust of time had only made them more beautiful. Perhaps Angelo reflected that he, with new stones, would do well only if he remembered the words of Jesus.

For three and a half years Padre Pio saw Angelo Lupi, at work at the construction site, every time he passed to and from the church. In summer Angelo worked in his shirt sleeves; he wore a rain coat casually thrown over his shoulders when it rained; he stood in the snow in thin-soled, low-cut shoes, indifferent to the cold. From time to time Angelo would turn his head toward the church, and smile briefly at Padre Pio.

By early October of 1949, he had cut avenues and ramps and clearings and driveways around the Fiorello La Guardia Clinic, and had designed raw material into a great pink building, with one hundred and fifty windows on the front wall. In this structure he had poured lime and cement and steel and lumber by thousands of tons. Beneath the building, in sheds and on the open ground, he had accumulated the other lime, cement, and stones that would go into parapets and pillars and archways. Great supplies of Ravenna, Carrara, Massa, Pisa, Volterra, and Carso marble, to be used in the halls and stairways and corridors, were piled up and ready to use. The only change noticeable in Angelo after his three and a half years of labor was that he looked more intent and determined than when he had first started.

From time to time, the people of San Giovanni Rotondo would say to the friars, "The architect says he will be finished in 1956, is that true?"

"Correct."

"But that is seven years from now. Just imagine if he were not capable and fast, imagine what would happen then." And they would turn and look at the architect, his determined and alert face, his neat crew-cut hair, his white shirt with the knit wool brown tie, his brown gabardine jacket which he had been wearing for three and a half years. The men spoke of Angelo with amazement and pride, the women with compassion, the monks with enthusiasm, Padre Pio with love.

Before daylight each morning, Angelo would have awakened the watchmen, and before the laborers arrived he would already have inspected the job. Throughout each day, Padre Pio would see him work in a sort of illuminating splendor. His confidence seemed boundless. For three and a half years now he had relied on Padre Pio entirely. He kept up with the stigmated priest a sort of mental dialogue, and it was this, rather than strength or training or intellectual effort, that kept him sure of his work.

On October 6, 1949, suddenly a little before twilight Angelo Lupi quit. He sat down on a drum, dropped his blueprints to the ground, and hung his head. Padre Pio had not appeared at the front door of the monastery, and he would not. Padre Pio had been struck by illness. It was a serious illness, with frighteningly high fevers.

The monks stood clustered about the front of the monastery, waiting for the doctors. They watched the architect, and saw that he could not resume his work. It was as if, because of Padre Pio's illness, Angelo thought the dialogue had been obstructed. The friars had sensed the dialogue for three and a half years. They saw that Angelo needed "his protection," needed it in fact as much as he needed breathing.

The architect sat as if he had been struck by a cataclysm. He did not move until the doctors and the people of San Giovanni Rotondo had gathered on the front of the monastery in the last of twilight. Then he rose and ordered the laborers to stand guard on the million dollars worth of equipment, to protect it against a swelling tide of crimes. Not only in town but in the whole country in general. Then Angelo approached the friars and the doctors. With something of despair in his voice, he asked, "How is he?" When he heard that the doctors were worried he turned to the monks. His speech was rapid and barely coherent. He talked of "pitiful personal talents," said that without "the power" the "well wishes," the "attention of God," his destiny on earth was left "so naked" as to make any further work on the House for the Relief of Suffering "impossible."

"Come with me," said Brother Gaudenzio. "Or better, go

with him," and he pointed to Brother Carmelo da Sessano, the thirty-eight-year-old monk who when he was still in his teens had known Padre Pio. Brother Carmelo was now the Guardian Brother.

"Let us go pray," said Brother Carmelo.

On October 7, newspapers announced to the world that Padre Pio was ill. They described the sorrow of San Giovanni Rotondo, mentioned the swelling number of pilgrims, and exclaimed at the impact of the news on all Italy. The illness, as the newspapers told of it, was a serious one. Doctors feared complications that might cause the death of the stigmated priest.

Pilgrims kept a long vigil. They stood in the clearing from October 7 to the morning of the ninth when they learned that Padre Pio was out of danger. Then, and not until then, the architect returned to his blueprints. His face looked sunken. He had not slept. He had prayed continuously with the friars. Angelo worked little and nervously until the end of November when, at last, Padre Pio was back in the confessional.

On December 9, 1949, another milestone was reached. The roof of the Fiorello La Guardia Clinic was completed. Gathered in the clearing for the ceremony of the completion of the roof were the Provincial Father of the Capuchin Order, Father Paolino di Casacalente, Archpriest Professor Principe representing the Bishop of Manfredonia, government representatives De Caro and De Meo, a Mr. Dayton, representing America, Major Raynolds, chief of the UNICEF mission, and the prefect of the province Donadu. Many of the clergymen and government officials had been at the 1947 ceremony of the first stone.

The *Gazetta del Mezzogiorno* of Bari, described the ceremony: "The guests and the authorities were received by the president of the Fiorello La Guardia clinic, Signor Sacchetti, the vice-president, Dr. Sanvico, the administrative delegate, Dr. Sanguinetti, the administrator, Dr. Kisvarday, and the architect and director of works, Angelo Lupi. During the ceremony, the architect laid down the last tile on the roof. Then the guests gathered in one of the enormous salons in the building. In their speeches, the government officials expressed their gratitude to Fiorello La Guardia and the other American officials who had helped with the initial cost of the clinic. Mr. Dayton praised the spirit of the Italian people for the virtues that, he said, were overcoming the difficulties of postwar Italy's hard-put economy."

Padre Pio welcomed the visitors in Saint Mary of the Graces. He spoke to them about his ideals for the hospital, the stipulation that it would have no wards. He repeated what he had said during the ceremony of the first stone, that the beautiful marble, though it was a luxury, was worthwhile because it would please the eye, and beauty is good for the sick.

Soon after the ceremony, Padre Pio returned to the confessional. Because of the great number of pilgrims that day, he was in the confessional until ten in the evening.

A little after ten the same evening, a young man stopped him in the *clausura* and said, "Padre Pio, you guided me through the desert. I am the son of the man. . . ."

"Yes," said Padre Pio. "I told your father that he should go and pray because you would be back home at the third moon."

Padre Pio put his hands on the boy's head. The young man was saying, "I had lost my squad in the desert, I was alone, but even so I made it out of the war and to Marseille and then to Corsica. When I arrived home and my father showed me your picture, I said, 'This is the monk who guided me through the desert.' "

"I have been praying for you ever since," answered Padre Pio. "I bless you. Go now."

The same kind of extraordinary phenomena that had first attracted so many pilgrims to Padre Pio continued, and perhaps even increased in number. On January 14, 1950, *Il Gazzettino*, a Venice daily newspaper, wrote: "An occurrence that seems like a miracle took place Tuesday morning at about ten o'clock, in a little country home near our city. The home is inhabited by Egidio and Rosa Sari with their sons and daughters. One of their children is a girl, Wanda, who was born on July 11, 1932. Wanda has been under medical care for two years. The nature of her illness is unspecified, but doctors have said it was caused by the failure of a gland in her brain to develop properly. For two years, Wanda has been constantly in a critical state, rendered particularly dangerous by the fact that she could not keep down any food. Lately she had been visited by a number of specialists, but to no avail.

"On Tuesday morning Wanda was in perfect health again. Her father, who had seen that medical efforts were not helping the girl, had turned to Padre Pio of Pietrelcina. On the morning of the tenth, Wanda had been delirious and weeping for some hours. Just before ten o'clock, Maria Catto Dal Ben entered her room, with a picture of Padre Pio, given to her by Lia Mattiuzzi. At the same time, some of Wanda's relatives, and some friends of the Sari family also entered the room. Wanda had just taken the picture of the Capuchin in her hands. Wanda says she immediately felt happy, and at once all her pains vanished. Overcome with joy, she screamed and wept. The people in her room, after the first few minutes of astonishment, embraced Wanda in delight. Wanda asked for some food, a request she had not made since her illness began. Without help from any one, Wanda was able to leave her bed, wash, and comb her hair. Soon after she returned to bed, in order to follow the command of Padre Pio who had appeared to her during her delirium and had told her that she should stay in bed for four days. Yesterday, when we saw Wanda, she appeared to be in perfect health, and in good spirits. We have reported scrupulously what happened. We will be able to give further details after Wanda is visited by doctors again. Because of what happened to Wanda, there have been a number of conversions in our city. The ecclesiastic authority has not made a pronouncement on Wanda's sudden change from crisis to good health."

The same newspaper published a second article on Wanda Sari on January 18, 1950, "We have visited Wanda Sari today. Her father and mother are not able to say much about the illness she had before she suddenly became well. They state only that they had turned to Padre Pio simply because med-

ical efforts had been futile. Wanda has told us, 'I saw Padre
Pio while I was having the fit, and I felt well. I felt I could
get up from bed, and I did. I washed and combed my hair
and time passed and I still was feeling very well. I still feel
very well now.'

"Wanda Sari left her home today for a walk in the sun. She
asserted once more that she feels well. But to see her, so thin,
in the big bed of her parents, the girl of the miracle seems to
suffer much. This is the fourth day since the miracle and she
went to bed only because Padre Pio told her 'not to leave her
bed completely for four days.' Her mother told us, 'Wanda
knows many beautiful things, but she keeps them to herself.'
All we could do was to look at Wanda. She was smiling. We
report a statement from the pharmacist, Carli Manfred, who
wrote to us as follows: 'I am glad to be able to furnish data
on Wanda Sari. Dr. Fortunato Sordoni, of Oderzo, has ad-
vised that Wanda should be brought to Treviso, and be visited
for some eighteen days by Dr. Enrico Azzi. After the instantaneous cure her parents wished to take her to Treviso,
but they are poor and have postponed the trip. Her doctor,
Dr. Sordoni, has been trying to help her for two years. She
was paralyzed, and she could not keep down any food. I have
filled many prescriptions, and I have often spoken to the
doctor, who always told me he could not do much for Wanda
Sari.' "

On April 22, 1951, the *Giornale dell' Emilia* published an
article signed by G. C. Zanfrongnini, on the miracle of Marina
Zanotti di Carpi. "*Palazzo Pitti* is the name of a gray building

in the periphery of Modena. It is the home of derelicts, a great big room divided into cubicles, where often some ten and twelve people live crowded together. But for a few days now people have been turning to this home, looking up at a window in the apartment of the Fregni family. Here live twelve people, with only one bedroom for the family. They were eleven until a few days ago, but then a cousin, Marina Zanotti, came to live with them. Marina is seventeen years old. She was crippled, paralyzed in one leg and one arm. Doctors had tried to do something for her for two years. From the window of the Fregni family today, a special ray of sunlight seems to shine—a light such that it seems to illuminate the whole home. The girl Marina has suddenly become well. It happened from evening to morning, after a mystical apparition.

"It is this vision which sets afire the imagination, even of those who are very skeptical. The girl says. . . . 'A blue drape came closer and closer to me the other evening while I was going to bed. At first I was frightened and so I tried to hide under the blankets. Then I heard a sweet voice: *Do not fear, have faith, rise and walk because your leg is well.*'

"Marina continues: 'That suddenly, I did not believe the voice, but now I regret my doubt. In the morning, when I usually get up, I pushed my leg out of bed, put the foot on the floor, and I was able to stand on my foot. I found it easy to walk, on my leg which before could not hold me up. I was walking like all the other girls. And I could move my arm. I could move my hand. I could move my fingers. My fingers were paralyzed for two years. Now they were moving as I wished them to, and with my fingers I could pick up whatever object I wished to pick up.'

"As she spoke, Marina went to a drawer from which she took the photograph of Padre Pio of Pietrelcina, signed to her. The photograph had been given to Marina a few days before her miraculous cure by two friends who had gone to San Giovanni Rotondo. Padre Pio had spoken to Marina's friends, assuring them that he would bless Marina and pray for her. Marina now says that next summer she will go to San Giovanni Rotondo to meet Padre Pio in person. As she speaks of Padre Pio her eyes are luminous with joy.

"Marina's aunt, a massive housewife with an unemployed husband and unemployed sons and daughters, says, 'I did not believe in anything. I believed in nothing. I was a beast without faith, without soul, without hope in my gray poverty. But Marina has brought in faith. If I had read of the miracle I would not have believed it, yet it has happened, it has happened to Marina. People around here say that Marina is in secret agreement with the priests in order to frighten poor folks with this talk of miracles. But talk to my sons who have not been brought up by priests, and still they will tell you that there has been a miracle. We have never been people to go to church every day, but now, because of what has happened, we cannot restrain ourselves.'

"Marina has told us that when she was eight years old her father died of consumption. Her family has always been poor, and full of suffering. Her mother has done all kinds of work to support the children. Her brother, Giuseppe, was killed at the age of twenty by Germans, during a raid in Carpiginao.

Soon after, Marina became ill, and began to go from hospital to hospital, submitting herself to all sorts of cures and experiments. None were of any use. Two months ago her aunt offered to give her a home in the gray and poor *Palazzo Pitti*. Her family did not want her to suffer in hospitals any longer, and the doctors said there was nothing they could do for Marina. When she came to her aunt, she would look out of the window, and watch the other girls of her age walk and use their arms. She would often dream of her brother, the one killed by the Germans. He would say in the dream that she should not lose hope.

"Now Marina is well. After we visited her, she walked with us in the courtyard. All the people there were staring at Marina, the girl they call 'the miracle.' "

In July 2, 1951, *Il Giornale di Sicilia* published an article concerning the sudden cure of Camillo Lo Monaco ". . . from attacks which doctors could not explain. Lo Monaco was suffering from gastric ulcer and colic, but his seizures were such that doctors could not say for certain that those particular sicknesses were the cause of them. The fits were severe, and made Camillo Lo Monaco delirious. Maria Lo Monaco, his wife, wrote a letter about her husband to Padre Pio, and in his answer, Padre Pio told her to insist in her prayers. Padre Pio enclosed two pictures, one of Brother Raffaele of St. Elia a Pianisi, the other of the Madonna of the Graces. Camillo Lo Monaco, in his delirium, kept repeating, 'I see a monk without his head.' His wife told him that was Brother Raffaele of St. Elia a Pianisi, whose skull is on the main altar of that church. During her prayer, Maria Lo Monaco heard a voice: 'One who is dead can still be alive,' said the voice. At this moment her husband in disconnected words was saying that he had dreamed of the Brother without the head gripping the railing of the Gancia church in Palermo. He could see the monk, but not his head. Maria wrote again to Padre Pio. On the same day that she wrote the second letter, relatives came to visit the sick man. One of them had a Crucifix blessed by Padre Pio, and they took the crucifix into Camillo's room. One of the sons opened the window. He said, 'Do you smell this odor of roses? This is the odor I smelled when Padre Pio was close to me, as I was kissing his hand.'

"A short while later, the doctor arrived. He examined Camillo, and said he was between life and death. A heart specialist, who came a few minutes later, said that Camillo's heart was hardly functioning because of hemorrhage. He would die, the specialist told the relatives, in a few minutes. Camillo Lo Monaco was mumbling about the perfume of roses. He was out of danger that night, and sitting up in bed the next morning. He had a heart lesion, as the heart specialist affirmed. The doctors frankly spoke of a miracle."

The Rome *Giornale d'Italia,* published the following article on September 8, 1951. "Dr. Novelli received us in his office to answer questions about Ulisse Santini, who was on his deathbed a few days ago and now is well again. Ulisse is 'the Santini of the miracle' of whom everybody in the zone of Piazza Vescovio speaks these days. Dr. Sandro Novelli told us: 'I visited the Signor Santini in February of 1950, and at that time I noticed a lowering of his voice. For this reason I sent him to Regina Elena clinic. My fears were unfortunately well founded, because the railroad station master Santini had a form of epitheliosis of the vocal cords. Because he was also severly anemic, he lost a great deal of weight in a few weeks. In order to avoid a heart collapse, I gave him injections. But one heart attack was followed by another, until finally, he was in coma. Still I continued to give him injections in an effort to prolong his vegetative life. The morning of February 1, the parish priest of the Piazza Vescovio church, Don Cesare, phoned me about Santini. He told me he would like to be the priest to deliver the last rite. I called the Santini family, although I knew that the railroad station master had not been very much of a church goer. However, the family agreed. At five o'clock Santini had Communion. One hour later, as I sat by the patient's bedside, I heard crying from another room of the house. I opened the bedroom door and stepped out. Signora Santini came to me, talking about a miracle. She said she had seen Padre Pio of Pietrelcina by the bedroom door. When I went back into the bedroom, Signor Santini sat up in bed. His general condition was suddenly normal. He drank soup and ate a slice of bread. The patient, who had been in coma, was perfectly well in three weeks."

On February 15, 1952, the *Giornale dell' Emilia*, a Bologna daily paper, published an article with the title: "Sudden cure of an old man who invoked Padre Pio."

"Early this morning people in Forlimpopoli began talking about a miracle. For seven years, people have been seeing

Severino Naldi, seventy years old, in a wheelchair. Every day
his wife would push the wheelchair in the streets of the little
town. This morning they saw Naldi on his feet, taking a walk
in the street in front of his house. Severino Naldi told them
calmly that he had received a blessing from Padre Pio, and
that Padre Pio had cured him. We have spoken today with
Naldi. He told us 'Last year, on the eighth of December, the
feast of the Blessed Virgin, I had the inspiration to write a
letter to Padre Pio. I asked him for blessing. For seven years,
I have been unable to leave my wheelchair. My doctor is
Caetano Morelli, head of the Ospedale Civico, and he has
been taking care of me all these years. When I wrote to Padre
Pio, because of humility, I did not ask him for a miracle. I
was writing more about my soul, and I asked him for spiritual
help. Two days after mailing the letter, I had a strange, new
feeling that I do not know how to describe. But when I went
to visit my little nephew, who is my thirteenth nephew, on
January 16, this year, I felt I could stand up from the wheelchair. As I was kissing my little nephew's hand, I remembered
that Padre Pio wears half-gloves, and at that very moment I
rose from the wheelchair.' "

The *Messaggero Veneto* published, on April 10, 1952, the
following article: "We visited Adele Minuissi di Fogliano today, because people of this town in the Carso mountain speak
of a miracle that happened to her through the intercession of
Padre Pio of Pietrelcina. The Signora Minuissi told us: 'Before
I became pregnant, I had a nervous breakdown, and it de-

stroyed my health. When my pregnancy began, I became very ill. Soon my condition was such that I could not leave my bed. I was in the care of four doctors. I went to a hospital, but they could not help me. The doctors told me I could not survive my pregnancy, and I was dismissed from the hospital to await my death at home. My friend, Laura Battistutta, began to pray, and to ask Padre Pio to help me. After fifteen days of prayers, Padre Pio appeared to my friend in a dream. In the dream, he told her how I should go through my labor. He said my child would be born on March 9, 1952, at five o'clock in the morning. He said to call the child Mario Pio. My friend said to Padre Pio in the dream, "But Adele does not believe," and Padre Pio answered: "She will believe." He also said that my child would have Cross marks on his wrists, and on his right shoulder. It all came true, the child was born on that day, at that hour, and the child had the marks on his left wrist and his right shoulder.'

"We have seen the statements of Signora Minuissi's doctor and of the nurse in the hospital, made when she was dismissed to go home to die. We have seen the statement of the midwife, about the hour of the child's birth. We have also spoken to the Signora's friend, Laura Battistutta, and to the priest of the village. It was obvious to us that the child was born through a miracle, because the medical statements we have read say that the mother was dying with *lipomatosis*. This disease affects the heart. We have seen the child, the marks on his left wrists, the marks on the right shoulder. He is a nice child, like all other children."

The *Giornale dell' Emilia*, published the following article
on December 10, 1953. "Last July, Annunziata Cremonini in
Morara, sixty-seven years old, recovered in the Saint Orsola
Hospital from an infection which later proved to have been
leukemia. Various blood transfusions were given her, but they
did not seem to help. Her son Marino put a picture of Padre
Pio under her pillow, and she suddenly recovered. The doctors were baffled. However, since leukemia can have periods
of pause, the doctors have waited until now before making
any statement. The complete recovery of Annunziata Cremonini has led the people of Gallo di Castel San Pietro to talk
about miracle."

The *Resto del Carlino* published, on April 6, 1954, the
following article: "It is not strange that a Sister would accompany a sick person hoping to be cured on a pilgrimage,
nor is it strange for the pilgrimage to be directed to the thau-
maturge Padre Pio of Pietrelcina. What is strange is the fact
that the Sister, herself a victim of an incurable disease, goes on
a long journey to help another person and returns from the
journey cured herself. This is the case of a fifty-two-year-old
nun, Sister Attilia Boninsegna. Sister Attilia is from Asparetto
di Cerca, but at present she lives in our city of Bologna with
the Little Sisters of the Sacred Family. Her special mission is
nursing at the San Domenico Section of the Ospedale Mag-
giore, in the piazza of the Tribunali. Sister Attilia has been in
our city for ten years. Thirty-eight years ago, Sister Attilia
suffered a spinal disorder called Pott's disease. Ever since, she

has had to wear an apparatus which she could remove only before going to bed at night. She was obliged to sleep on a very hard bed, to avoid having any motion at her spine.

"A few days ago, a woman affected with epilepsy asked Sister Attilia to accompany her to Padre Pio, in San Giovanni Rotondo. The Sister agreed. Padre Pio received them. The epileptic woman had a turn for the better, and Sister Attilia thought that her patient would soon be well. But this did not happen. However, Sister Attilia discovered, upon returning from San Giovanni Rotondo, that the apparatus she had worn for her spine would no longer fit around her as well as it had before she met and talked with Padre Pio. She began to hope. She spoke of her hope to the Sister Superior. Then she went to one of the doctors at the hospital and called the imperfect fit of the apparatus supporting her spine to his attention. Doctors gave her various radiologic examinations and discovered that, although her spine was still deformed, she was cured of the Pott's disease. She was also cured of some open infections in her left leg which were now closed. She has now returned to San Giovanni Rotondo, to thank Padre Pio for what she considers to be a blessing received through his intercession with the Lord."

With such works made known, pilgrims arrived daily in San Giovanni Rotondo in ever increasing numbers. They came to thank Padre Pio for his prayers and help, to hear his Mass, to be confessed by him and receive Holy Communion from him. They became a continuous flow that completely changed the face of San Giovanni Rotondo. By 1955, hotels and homes had been built close to the clearing in front of Saint Mary of the Graces.

The construction of the House for the Relief of Suffering had gone on with great speed since the day of the celebration of the roof. At the end of 1955, a little before Christmas, the House for the Relief of Suffering was complete, inside and out. It was equipped with five hundred beds, four beds to a room, and it had four fully modern surgery salons, a department for radiology, a pharmaceutical department. There was a library on the first floor, and on the second floor were surgery rooms for minor operations. The internal medicine departments were on the third floor, and on the fourth floor were the pediatric and obstetrical departments. There was also a center for nurses' training and a section for internes. The building, all air-conditioned, even housed a moving picture room. And of course, there was a chapel. Twenty-four doctors and eighty nurses had applied to work for the new hospital when it was ready to begin functioning.

Before Easter in 1956 the church of Saint Mary of the Graces was also partly rebuilt. The front of the church was extended leftward up to the front door of the monastery. The old door was left intact, but three new doors were built in the extension, on the left side of the church's main entrance, and three doors were added on the right side, the side closest to the Fiorello La Guardia Clinic. The front of the church was lifted over the level of the bell tower, with four segments of roof centered by a statue of the Madonna. An arched window was carved out beneath the statue, and nine high and narrow

decorative openings flanked the new window. Before the renewal the group of buildings, church and monastery, presented the semblance of farm houses. Now the church had a
trim entrance but the monastery was left as of old.

The sight of both the renewed church and the House for
the Relief of Suffering offered pilgrims arriving from a world
that produced more suffering than bread and wine, a new
world, a world of beauty and wonder.

With the hospital to start functioning soon, one would sup-
pose that Padre Pio's concern with the many sick who still
came to him would be lessened. He could, after all, advise
them to wait until the clinic was ready, and then simply rely
on the doctors and nurses there. This, however, it was not in
Padre Pio's nature to do.

Dr. Giovanni Gigliozzi was a well known radio commen-
tator in Italy. He knew Padre Pio well and loved him dearly.
Dr. Gigliozzi was a member of the organization that collected
funds for the House for the Relief of Suffering. In April of
1956, his family physician in Rome, where he lived, told him
that his mother had cancer. Mrs. Gigliozzi would have to
undergo drastic surgery.

Giovanni Gigliozzi was crushed by the news. But he was a
man of unshakable faith, a quiet and kind and generous person,
always eager to help friends and strangers. Now, he considered the idea of asking a favor for himself of Padre Pio. He
knew he could rely on Padre Pio's sympathy, yet he was re-
luctant to impose on his friend. Instead, he decided to wait
until his mother had had further tests. But when the terrible

news was confirmed beyond a doubt, Giovanni Gigliozzi could no longer endure keeping silent. He needed to talk with Padre Pio, and to receive from him the courage he would need to face the ordeal of his mother's operation. So he set out for San Giovanni Rotondo. He thought his mother could be cared for in the new hospital, which was to open in a matter of weeks.

In his sorrow he felt the journey by car to be endless. He knew that it would have seemed even longer by train. He drove down to the shores of Gaeta, then eastward through the hills and north across the hills, then past the flat land of Foggia and through town and up the mountains. When he finally arrived, tired and low-spirited, late in the evening, he went straight to the Hotel S. Maria delle Grazie.

The utter quiet began to calm his mind. In the spotless, modern room, he stood at the window. The vast night sky was filled with stars. He reflected that he could have gone straight to Brother Carmelo da Sessano, the Superior, or to friends, since he had many friends in San Giovanni Rotondo. But he felt suddenly grateful to life in general and to his fate to be in the peaceful room, alone. He decided to speak to the doctors in the morning about admitting his mother to the new clinic. He felt reassured.

He went to bed expecting to sleep well, but he was unable to close his eyes. The dogs in nearby farmhouses, dogs up and down the shoulder of the mountain, and in the courtyards of the homes near the monastery, were barking constantly. He rose and pulled in the window shutters. The barking was just as loud. He could not shut it out. At last he fell into a restless sleep. He was up early, for Mass. Later he spoke briefly with Brother Carmelo.

"I will tell Padre Pio you are here," said Brother Carmelo.

Padre Pio spoke to Giovanni as the sun was coming up. "Listen to me, Giovanni. Your mother knows that I will pray for her."

Perhaps it was the tone of Padre Pio's voice that made Giovanni's heart leap with hope. His eyes filled with tears. He went to church and knelt and thanked God. Later in the day he saw Padre Pio again, as the priest passed through the church to the confessional. Padre Pio nodded to him slightly in a friendly way of greeting.

There was nothing more to be said, so Giovanni began the trip back to Rome. As he drove, he tried to define and clarify his feelings. Since he had spoken with Padre Pio, he had not thought of his mother's operation again. He could not find words to describe the illumination of spirit that he felt as he was driving back to Rome.

At home he said quietly to his mother as he sat at her bedside, "We should not worry. In a few days. . . ."

"What did he say?" asked the mother.

"He said he will pray. We know, he prays for us."

At Mrs. Gigliozzi's next medical examination, which took place a week later, the doctors did not find the malignant tumor.

"There is nothing," the doctors said. "It has vanished."

Giovanni and his mother did not utter a word. They left the clinic and went down to the car and started out for San Giovanni Rotondo.

The Fiorello La Guardia Clinic was inaugurated on May 5, 1956. Fifteen thousand people stood on the twelve-acre grounds of the House for the Relief of Suffering. Before he stepped out of Saint Mary of the Graces, Padre Pio delivered to his doctor friends the theme of the ceremony, speaking quietly to a small group: "Your mission is to cure the sick, but if you do not bring love to the bedside of the suffering I do not believe that medicines are very useful. I have experienced this. My doctor, when in 1916 and 1917 I was sick, brought me first of all a word of comfort. Love cannot do without the Word. How can you express love if not with words which lift the ill spiritually? Later I went to a specialist who, without too much fuss, told me that I was consumptive and that, at the most, I had one more year to live. I returned home with death in my heart, resigned to the will of God. And, as you see, I am still here. The prophecy of the specialist did not come true. But not all the sick are like Padre Pio of 1916 and 1917. Bring God to the sick. That will have more value than any medicine."

Padre Pio stepped out of Saint Mary of the Graces to say Mass on a temporary altar erected in front of the hospital. During the Mass, despite the number of people, the worshippers attended with a devotional silence.

At the beginning of the inaugural ceremony, military planes from the Manfredonia air base flew overhead, as if for a national ceremony. Seated before the front door of the House for the Relief of Suffering were church and government officials, both from Italy and from many other countries. Padre Pio sat between the Father General of the Capuchin

Order and Giacomo Cardinal Lercaro of Bologna. In the front row of seats, with Padre Pio, were the Bishop of Manfredonia, Monsignor Cesarano, Bishops of other regions, Vatican City officials, officials of the Italian government, and the heads of the Fiorello La Guardia Clinic. Among the distinguished doctors attending the ceremony was Paul Dudley White, President Eisenhower's cardiologist.

His Eminence Giacomo Cardinal Lercaro suggested that Padre Pio should speak at the microphone. Padre Pio shook his head, but since Cardinal Lercaro's heart was set on the idea, Padre Pio rose and took the two, three steps to the microphone to say a few words: "We are promptly answering the call of God. One step has been taken. Let us not slow down, myself in ceaseless prayer, as a useless servant of Jesus Christ . . ." At one point Padre Pio supported himself up by holding onto Brother Carmelo da Sessano, and it seemed that he would faint. His eyes were filled with tears.

After Padre Pio had opened the ceremony, other speakers took his place at the microphone. Dr. Paul Dudley White concluded his address with, "I go back to America deeply moved by the realization of this great project inspired by Padre Pio."

The well-known French specialist, Professor Evans, concluded his speech with the words: "I bring to Padre Pio the admiration of Paris and all of France. . . ."

Padre Pio turned to Brother Carmelo and whispered, "But where is Angelo?" Here were people praising his work, his architectural inspiration, and Angelo Lupi seemed to be nowhere about. Brother Carmelo answered in a whisper, "I think I see him, though I am not sure, in back with Pietruccio." Pietruccio was the blind postman of San Giovanni Rotondo who had stood by the architect, as though advising him, for ten years.

The president, vice-president, and administrators of the Fiorello La Guardia Clinic described Padre Pio's determination, that had imparted to them the courage to be bold in the realization of the project. Dr. Baise, director of the hospital, spoke of the hospital policy. The bills of the poor would be paid by funds. One of the first of these funds was established by Mario Gambino, the Waldorf Astoria cook. Another was set up by Beniamino Gigli, the singer.

At the conclusion of the ceremony people were invited to visit the Fiorello La Guardia Clinic, which was officially opened and could now start receiving patients. The fifteen thousand people began to form lines to the main doors, and as they entered the twenty-four doctors and eighty nurses guided them through the chapel, library, moving-picture hall, medical and surgical facilities, the department for infantile paralysis, the radiologic department, and the hospital rooms.

The whole project had cost five million dollars.

Chapter 13

PILGRIMS WHO WALK the little distance from Saint Mary of the Graces to visit the House for the Relief of Suffering today go through gardens landscaped on the front and to the sides of the magnificent building. Pilgrims can also drive up from the clearing in front of the church, along wide ramps that lead to the hospital. Pilgrims say, "It is a city in itself." And former patients say, "It has the best doctors there are."

The church is too small and it is always crowded. The monastery and church stand today on the same ground they occupied of old, and the cobbled clearing in front of Saint Mary of the Graces is as it has always been. As of old, pilgrims say, "Yes, Padre Pio makes miracles."

New Pilgrims, who come for the first time, soon understand the world they are in. As they look at the hospital they seem to sense the spirit of the stigmated priest who is now seventy-three years old, the spirit alive with prayer, charity, and love. They believe that his prayers brought the pink stones needed to construct the House for the Relief of Suffering up the mountain, one by one.

Those who know the South understand Padre Pio best. They understand why Padre Pio, searching deep in the pocket

of his robe, took out a gold coin as the first offer for the
project of the hospital. They understand that in other respects
as well he is still a son of the South. They see it in his use of
dialect, his devotion to the saints and his prayers for the protection of the Madonna, his reliance on the Gospel, his meals
of fresh vegetables, his quiet monastery.

If pilgrims know the South that well, then they understand
Padre Pio perfectly when he speaks to them of the life of
Christians. "The life of a Christian is an unceasing reaction
against himself and produces beauty at the price of sorrow.
Until you fear, you will not sin," Padre Pio says. "Man is
made of such pride that when he is rich and has health he
believes himself to be a God, if not altogether superior to God
Himself, but when a thing happens toward which he and
people like him are powerless, then he remembers that there
is a Supreme Being."

When the singer Beniamino Gigli visited Padre Pio and
offered to sing for him, Padre Pio asked to hear a Neapolitan
song, and the pilgrims learned with that song that the South
is also a land of poetry. "Yes, the more primitive a village is
in these parts," say the pilgrims, "the better it can dream. It is
strange."

They have come to Saint Mary of the Graces through
Amalfi and Capri and Ravello and Sorrento and Positano and
Taormina and Ischia, and on the long journey they have
learned about that strangeness.

Pilgrims meet Padre Pio in the confessional, and then gather
in groups in the clearing. They talk. "I had the opportunity
to speak with him in the sacristy yesterday and when I mentioned his diet, saying that he should eat more, he answered

me, 'I have never eaten much, why should I start now in my old age?' "

The pilgrims talk to the doctors they meet between church and hospital. They ask, "Doctor, tell us, what does he think of science?" And the doctors answer, "He has always said: 'I firmly believe in medical science.' "

The pilgrims ask Padre Pio, "What do you do in the hospital?"

"Do not be surprised about my presence here," he answers, "for my mission is in fact that of consolation, the consolation of those who suffer, especially those whose spirits suffer. I know that you seek eagerly two things: happiness, and truth—that is, God. The first thing you seek is impossible, not only for you, but for anyone else, because the earth is a valley of tears where each bears his Cross, so that, in short, happiness is not of this world. The second thing, that is, God, you can find if you want, but at the moment you are on the wrong path, one of falsehood and vanity. It is not science that can give you the One Who is. Science, even at its greatest, is a small thing. It is less than nothing compared to the formidable mystery of the Divinity. You must take another path. Drop passions from your heart and humble yourself in dust, and pray. In this manner you will surely find God—serenity, and peace in this life and eternal beatitude in that other life. I have spoken. I go now because others who suffer wait for consoling words. Jesus be praised."

And so, as a part of the South and a part of all places where "others who suffer wait for consoling words," to thousands of pilgrims Padre Pio belongs twice.

And new pilgrims come to San Giovanni Rotondo from the

226 of the earth. They start asking questions about

four corners of the earth. They start asking questions about Padre Pio even as they begin their journey, and receive loving answers from the heights of the Alps to the shores facing Africa. But it is from Rome down that people, like the four, five women of San Giovanni who have not missed Padre Pio's Mass since 1918, give familiar answers. Here people speak of miracles with glowing faith. "I had consumption," says the gasoline station owner in Giardinetto, seventy-five miles west of Foggia, "and last year I went to Padre Pio and look at me now. How do I look, eh?" Close to Foggia everyone mentions Padre Pio every day. Here, new pilgrims can approach any man and discover that the man carries with him a picture of Padre Pio. "Here he is, this is Padre Pio. And this Crucifix was blessed by Padre Pio."

And closer to San Giovanni Rotondo, in the land of the pink prickly-pears, the next man new pilgrims talk to says, "Communism would have been here long ago, except that Padre Pio started the hospital and folks have been working ever since."

The closer they travel, the more the new pilgrims learn that Padre Pio is intimately involved in the lives of the little people. From Foggia on they find that all the people have met Padre Pio face to face and have been blessed by him, "He put his hands on my head," the people say with a sudden illumination in their eyes. And pilgrims begin to feel that the whole South is involved in the destiny of Padre Pio.

Then, at one point, not too many miles east of Foggia on the highway, the sun-scorched heaviness of the flat lands begins to recede. Suddenly at the sight of the junction road sided with flowers, pilgrims find that the weariness of the long journey has vanished from them and the scenery before their eyes has become one of peaceful beauty. It is mountain beauty. As they start to climb the twisting flower-sided road, it is as if the texture of the sunlight and the feel of the air were lightened, although the flat lands of Puglie are still close behind. Then there are no more people about and the silence is complete. The new pilgrims say, "It is different here."

Now they are close to the stigmated priest who, quietly in his cell, takes the blood-soaked linen from his side and replaces it with a new linen, removes the blood-stained bandages from his hands and feet to bandage them over again with new gauze.

The pilgrims are now close. Now all at once worrisome entanglements fall away from the pilgrims. The scenery is that of Sunday morning, and the silence about is a Sunday morning silence.

The new pilgrims meet the four, five women on the way, wrapped in black shawls, with prayer book and beads, and men with their jackets over their shoulders, and they ask, "How far is San Giovanni Rotondo?"

"This is it."

"We mean the monastery," answer the pilgrims, who have stopped in the piazza.

"Up that way," say the people of San Giovanni Rotondo. "Up that way is Padre Pio."

The pilgrims feel the intimacy between these people and Padre Pio by the tone of their voices when they speak his name.

In a little while they can see the Fiorello La Guardia Clinic, and beneath it, gardens like the Tuilleries of the Louvre. And there is the clearing with its white-gray cobbles, there is the elm tree, the little wall beneath the tree, pilgrims grouped around buses and cars, pilgrims sitting on the wall beneath the elm. This side of the clearing there are the hotels and homes, and beyond it there is Saint Mary of the Graces and the monastery with its whitewash and gray front door.

This, for the new pilgrims, is an arrival in far distances.

There are good hotels and restaurants. There are homes with courtyards full of flowers. There are people who have lived here all their life. There are hundreds of pilgrims. There is the monastery and church and hospital and doctors in white jackets walking the ramps and driveways and gardens. There are monks moving from church to hospital.

The newcomers mingle with the other pilgrims. Those who understand Italian and those who do not find that there is no difference between them, for language is of little moment in this place. The rich and the poor, here, are as one, for in Saint Mary of the Graces there are no preferential arrangements.

How does Padre Pio manage in winter, with no heat in the monastery and so little food to provide natural warmth? How does he manage to kneel for so many hours in the night? The pilgrims ask the people of the region. And they ask how those who come in winter manage to reach Saint Mary of the Graces when they have to clear a path in the high snow. For answer, there is only faith and courage and love—the kind of faith, courage, love that emanate from the spirit of Padre Pio.

The spirit of the stigmated priest seems indeed to span the whole southern region visible along the chain of hills down to the arch of sea of Manfredonia.

The new pilgrims enter the church. There by the front door, there is the confessional, and in front and to the sides of it there are people kneeling and standing, all faces turned in one direction. There is Padre Pio. He is sitting in the confessional box. And suddenly the rest of the world vanishes and the new pilgrims, feeling detached from that world, stand and stare at the bearded face with the wide forehead and the moving lips. They gaze long at his covered palms, the fragile looking fingers opening and closing the confessional doors. The pilgrims stare long into his eyes.

For all who come to him, Padre Pio has prayers and words of comfort. To the sick, the troubled, the harassed souls who find themselves beset by doubt and uncertainty, he gives a message as simple as it is profound.

"Listen here," Padre Pio says. "As a child, when you sat at your mother's feet on a small stool, what did you see of her embroidery? From the wrong side you saw nothing that you could make out and understand, zig zag lines, threads this way and that. It made no sense to you at all. You were sitting on a low stool. You were looking at the embroidery from the wrong side. All the threads were confused in your eyes, and so you asked your mother what she was doing, what design, what pattern. You asked, 'Mother, may I know?' And you said, 'I can't make it out.' To answer you then, your mother lowered the embroidery, turning it for you to the right side. Then you were able to see the design and finally you understood it.

So, there. We see the wrong side of the work because we are sitting on a low stool."

The people who have come to the stigmated priest understand.

As they kneel for confession Padre Pio says, "Lean on the Cross like the Virgin Mary and you will not be without comfort. Mary was petrified before the Crucified Christ, but you cannot say that she was abandoned. She was loved better then, when she could not even cry." The pilgrims, rich or poor, crippled or healthy, begin to feel that they will rise and take home with them something beyond the riddle of tears, take it out of Saint Mary of the Graces back on the long road and down the steep mountain. They know that it is this something that they need, and have needed and will need, this something that is the certainty that they are loved better when they cannot even cry.

Bibliography

I monili dello Sposo, Vita di P. Pio da Pietrelcina, Giovanni Gigliozzi.
Centro Volontari della Sofferenza
Piazza Monte Savello 9, Roma.
Tipografia dei Monasteri—Subiaco (Roma)
Imprimatur: Sublaci, die Novembris 1958.
  Aloysius Aegidius Cavazzi O.S.B.
  Abbas Ordin. Coadiutor
  Visto: nulla osta
  Subiaco, 15 Ottobre 1958
  P.D. Paolo Carosi O.S.B.
  Revisore eccl.
*Per la Storia, Padre Pio di Pietrelcina, il primo
Sacerdote Stigmatizzato,* Alberto Del Fante.
Premiato Stab Tipografico Cav. Luigi Cappetta & F.
Foggia—1955.
Il Vero Volto di Padre Pio, M. Winowska. Edizioni Paoline
Titolo originale dell 'opera: Le Vrai Visage du
Padre Pio, pretre et Apotre, Libraire Artheme
Fayard—81 Rue du Saint-Gothard—Paris, 1955
Nulla Osta: Modena, 20–2–1956—D. Anegelo Bellanzon
Rev. eccl.
Imprimatur: Modena 21–2–1956—Can. Avito Biagi, Vic.
Generale

About the Author

Born in the South of Italy, Oscar De Liso is noted for his authentic, moving representations of life in that region. He studied belles-lettres at the University of Turin and at New York University. He first came to America at the age of three, but spent many years of his childhood in Italy. Returning to America in 1936 after an absence of nine years, at the age of twenty he discovered he had to relearn the English language. He received emphatic literary acclaim for *God's Thumb Down*, published in 1949. His second novel, *Wheat of Night*, followed in 1950 and was termed a "brilliant successor." Mr. De Liso's varied literary activities include free-lance writing and editing, and news editing for Ansa News Agency. He has also taught Italian at Stanford University. He lives in Nyack, New York.